Pete

# Th

Legacy of

# James E. Hanger,
# Civil War Soldier

Churchville Cavalry, CSA

By Bob O'Connor

The Amazing Legacy of James E. Hanger, Civil War Soldier

ISBN 978-0-7414-9993-6

Printed in the United States of America

This book is historical fiction, based on the true account of Mr. Hanger's remarkable life.

Published January 2014

INFINITY PUBLISHING
1094 New DeHaven Street, Suite 100
West Conshohocken, PA 19428-2713
Toll-free (877) BUY BOOK
Local Phone (610) 941-9999
Fax (610) 941-9959
Info@buybooksontheweb.com
www.buybooksontheweb.com

# Other books by the author

"The Perfect Steel Trap Harpers Ferry 1859"

"The Virginian Who Might Have Saved Lincoln"

"Catesby: Eyewitness to the Civil War"

"The U. S. Colored Troops at Andersonville Prison"

"The Centennial History of Ranson WV -- 1910 – 2010"

"The Life of Abraham Lincoln As President"

"A House Divided Against Itself"

"The Return of Catesby"

"Countdown to West Virginia Statehood"

www.boboconnorbooks.com

author@boboconnorbooks.com

Infinity Publishing ©2013

Cover Photograph -- www.theintermountain.com

# Dedication

To the more than 1.7 million persons in this country
who have had amputations for whatever reason,
including but certainly not limited to,
the brave military personnel
who help keep this country free

# Foreword

In all my studies of the American Civil War, I have often asked people whom I meet "who is the most significant soldier of the Civil War"? Although many names have been mentioned, not one person has ever come up with the name on the front of this book -- James E. Hanger.

I found James E. Hanger in my travels to sell my books at the Blue and Gray Reunion in Philippi, West Virginia. An event on their annual brochure listed several times over the weekend was the reenactment of the Hanger amputation. My first thought was "gross." I laughed at how I pictured in my mind that event would take place.

But when I got to the reunion, I found the Hanger amputation not gross at all, but, in fact, it was educational, historically significant, and informative. What I learned that day made me want to learn more.

The criteria I used to choose this soldier as the most significant Civil War soldier is the difference that James E. Hanger is still making **today**, more than 150 years later. Today, no other Civil War soldier is still in the forefront of American ingenuity, progress, and personal development as much as James E. Hanger. His amazing legacy was accomplished even though he was a soldier for less than two days. James E. Hanger is unknown to most everyone, including many of those people who are able to walk and move about because of this man's determination, craftsmanship, and dedication.

I hope after you read this book, James E. Hanger will be a soldier who will no longer be unknown. His story is too important to go untold.

# Setting the Scene
## Churchville, Virginia 1861

James Edward Hanger was born on February 25, 1843 at his parents' homestead, Mount Hope, in Churchville, Virginia, in Augusta County, just west of Staunton. His parents were William Alexander Hanger (who died in 1848 when James was 5 years old) and Elize Hogshed Hanger. His parents had been married on October 10, 1825. They had ten children. James E. Hanger was their 9th child and their 6th son.

The ten Hanger children and their birth dates were: Martha Obedience, 1826; Catherine J., 1828; George Alexander., 1830; William D., 1832; David W., 1834; John M., 1836; Anne Eliza, 1838; Henry H., 1840; James E., 1843; and Alice C., 1846.

Augusta County in 1861 was a very active county, providing food to the Tidewater area of Virginia. The local farmers grew corn, wheat, rye, and oats. Orchards and vineyards had sprung up throughout the area. Mills, distilleries, blacksmith shops, cooper shops, and foundries were prevalent. The railroad at Staunton, the newly completed Howardville and Rockfish Turnpike, and the Valley Turnpike provided a feeder system (some of which was macadamized) to take products to and from nearby markets.

Churchville had become a stage coach stop on those roads. Travelers stopped frequently at the Dudley House (now the Buckhorn Inn) and the Middle River Hotel to enjoy music, dancing, drinking, fine food, overnight accommodations, and gambling. The Dudley House's most famous traveler was probably Thomas J. Jackson (soon to be famous as General Thomas J. "Stonewall" Jackson) and his wife (who was the daughter of Dr. Junkin, President of Washington College) who stayed at the Dudley House in the Spring of 1854. Elize, James E. Hanger's mother, was the hotel keeper of the Middle River Hotel. She married Henry Eidson in 1858 and moved into the town of Churchville.

Jedediah Hotchkiss and his brother, Nelson, had founded the Loch Willow Academy School for Boys in the town a few years earlier.

There was a sizeable German population in town and several Lutheran and Reformed Churches. The Hanger ancestors were Germans and Hungarians who migrated to the Shenandoah Valley. Those folks had names like Hungerer and Hengerer that had been changed to Hanger.

Two prominent newspapers from Staunton provided those who lived in Churchville with the news of the region and with opposing views on the political climate. *The Staunton Spectator* was a pro-Union newspaper while *The Staunton Vindicator* was very pro-slavery and pro-secession.

An annual subscription to *The Staunton Spectator* that was published weekly was two dollars and fifty cents and could be paid by hauling good wood to the publisher's office if you didn't have the cash.

A recent study showed that about one-fifth of the county residents owned slaves even though the local farms, compared to those in the Tidewater area, tended to be smaller and therefore didn't require as many slaves to operate. Sixteen percent of the county's slave owners owned between ten and nineteen slaves while another thirty-two percent owned two or less. The Hanger family were among the Augusta county residents who owned slaves.

Some of the foundries, distilleries, and mills operated with slave labor while the rest of the local slaves worked on small farms. Often in this area, slaves were rented out to work away from their home base, creating fears in the community of insurrection similar to John Brown's event in Harpers Ferry less than two years previously. The county's 811 slave owners owned 5,617 slaves.

In Churchville in 1861, a farmer could purchase slave insurance for "reasonable rates and terms of one to three years" from several large insurance agencies in nearby Staunton.

As an aftermath to the election of Abraham Lincoln in late 1860, Augusta County voted to send three representatives to the state's convention to decide whether the Commonwealth of Virginia would follow their Southern neighbors and secede from the Union. The Augusta County representatives elected to attend that Richmond convention were Alexander H. Stuart, George Baylor, and John B. Baldwin – all pro-Union men.

When the final secession vote was taken on April 17, the Commonwealth of Virginia voted 88 to 55 in favor of secession. All three of the Augusta County delegates voted against secession.

Mt. Hope – Hanger home just outside of Churchville
House has been torn down
Photo by James Frederick Cook
Provided by James F. Cook III

# Chapter 1
## School Days at Washington College

April, 1861

My name is James Edward Hanger. I am from Churchville and an engineering student at Washington College in Lexington, Virginia and in my second year of school.

During my first term, I had to learn the legacy of the school. It had been founded as Liberty Hall Academy. In 1813, due to a $20,000 endowment given to the school by George Washington, it was renamed in his honor. Today a statue of the "Father of our Country", who we students disrespectfully called "Old George", stands tall atop the Colonade.

The all-boys school appealed to me because of my interest in engineering. I was always mechanically inclined. My long range plan was to complete school with a degree, but with the impending war, I doubted my future as a student.

And while the students were mostly pro-secession, our school leaders, including the college President, Dr. Junkin, who was a Presbyterian minister and a handful of teachers, tended to be pro-Union. That was most likely because they all had moved here from the North.

Dr. Junkin, the most vocal of the staff, made known his views by saying "the Union was always the master in the minds of American patriots; that Union was the basis of all their actions; that without Union there could be no freedom, no national government, and no independence."

As the days went by, talk about the war intensified. Students carried pro-secession banners.

Junkin's actions one recent day were quite troubling. He grabbed a student's secessionist banner and set it on fire yelling "so perish all efforts to dissolve this glorious Union."

Some of the students had already signed up for the local militia company, the Liberty Hall Volunteers, so designated due to the original name for the school. I trained for a few weeks with the militia. My mother opposed my actual joining them. In fact, she did not like the idea of my service at all. But she did support the enlistment of my older brothers, George and Henry.

The students at the school were quite excited to learn in class today that the military forces of Charleston, South Carolina, one of the secession states, had bombed Fort Sumter and caused its surrender.

While we had often talked formally in our classes and informally at most other times about the impending war, we certainly were not prepared for war. We were students. We grew up in farming communities. We did all know how to shoot a musket. But normally we were shooting at animals like deer, squirrel, and the like. Going to war would be very, very different for all of us. Not even once did I ever shoot at something that had any inkling of shooting back at me. We all rode horses too, so a cavalry company made more sense to us than an infantry company.

I had not given much thought to what a war might be like. We just all knew we didn't care much for the northern states invading and forcing their will on us Virginians.

As far as James Hanger was concerned, the thought of killing someone or being killed was not to my liking at all. I was not a coward. But at this point I was not willing to march to the front of the line and lead a charge on some enemy fortification either.

I knew my two brothers, George, who was thirteen years older than me, and Henry, who was four years older than me, had already told mother that they were joining up to be part of the Churchville Cavalry. Henry told me he thought the cavalry may be gone only for about three months because the war was projected to be short in duration. To me, the whole idea sounded glamorous and exciting as he talked about it.

The school was in danger of closing as many of the students were leaving to enlist. And Dr. Junkin resigned when the war started and left the school.

When news of the event at Fort Sumter arrived in town, Miss Surrett and some of the local ladies were in the process of helping the local tailor, Mr. Arnold, make uniforms at the Odd Fellows Hall for the Churchville Calvary Company. *The Staunton Vindicator* was already encouraging women in the area to furnish blankets for the soldiers, and local farmers were asked to give a horse and a wagon to help the cause.

In spite of my mother's discouragement, I was eighteen years old, and still considering my options.

Washington College
www.encyclopediavirginia.com

# Chapter 2
## The Churchville Cavalry
## Leaves for War

May 13, 1861

Today people from a wide area came to Churchville to support the Churchville Cavalry, commanded by Captain Frank Sterrett as they were preparing to leave to join the war.

My mother, my sisters, and I went to give our regards to my brothers and my first cousin, William Hanger, who had also enlisted. My brother, George, had entered as a 2$^{nd}$ Lieutenant. My other brother, Henry, was a 3$^{rd}$ Sergeant. Henry and George both had some long established leadership ability too, practiced in our family home by bossing me and my sisters around.

The women in town hosted a picnic for the men and boys who had enlisted. There was plenty of food and drink for everyone. The demeanor of the crowd was a mixture of excitement and nervousness, for sure. Mr. Walker gave a rousing speech. He told the men how proud we all were of their company -- the Churchville Cavalry. His message included comparing the fifty three local men in the company to soldiers in the Revolutionary War who defended our country against the British. He enthusiastically told them that they were patriots, and that whatever happened to them individually or to their company, the people of Churchville would be eternally grateful.

Reverend Arnold from the Methodist Church wished the new recruits Godspeed. And he encouraged the crowd to bow their heads as he asked a blessing for the safe return of each and every soldier to their loved ones when their one year enlistments were concluded. And then he led a round of three cheers for the Churchville Cavalry.

There were sad farewells from the women who were their mothers, sisters, and sweethearts, and many teary eyes as the men and boys mounted their horses. I saw several women holding locks of hair as a memento of the day. To me there was just a little too much fuss from someone going off to a distant war that was projected to be short and over in no time. How bad could it be? Did the mothers think this would be the last time they ever saw their boys?

As the event ended, the soldiers doffed their hats and rode off toward the war in western Virginia. Along with my brothers and my cousin were some of my other friends from Churchville including Hugh Turk, Ben Houseman, George Sherman, David Reid, and John Mann.

May 16, 1861

In the next few days, I noticed a void. Many of the students of Washington College were gone. Those of us who were still here met and talked about our individual situations. I personally thought that even though school was important, that perhaps the school would not be here if we didn't stand up and defend our rights. Others thought the school would not survive if all of us students marched off to join the war.

Enlistment papers of James Hanger's brothers, Henry and George.

Fold3 7509107                    Fold3 7509091

6

# Chapter 3
## Joining the Churchville Cavalry

May 28, 1861

About two weeks after the picnic, I decided to join the Churchville Cavalry. I don't know why I hadn't decided earlier. Most every one of my friends from both town and school had already joined. I had thought at first school had been more important to me. But now I wanted to be with my brothers and the others. I was determined to do my part to protect my homeland from those aggressors from the North who were expected to invade our land soon.

The cavalry, I was told, was now located around Philippi, Virginia. That little village was about 125 miles to the northwest of Churchville.

My mother was not happy about my decision. When I got ready to leave, she held me so tight that I was not sure that she would ever let go. She cried. My sisters cried. I had to be careful not to show any tears because, after all, I was a man. I did not even look back as I walked down the lane from the house to meet up with the others.

Several of us hitched a ride on a hospital wagon headed to the front. It was a five day ride. But I was happy to not have to be walking that distance. We were all in high spirits as we bounced around onboard the wagon. The roads were hard as rock due to the lack of rain.

The wagoneer must have hit every single rut in the road. We joked that he was trying to dislodge us from the back of the wagon. Several of the boys actually fell out of the wagon and had to pick themselves up and run to catch up. I hung on for dear life.

We sang songs and told stories to pass the time. I'm pretty sure some of those stories of their exploits were at least slightly exaggerated. We were enthusiastic and happy to be on this new adventure, though admittedly we had no idea what the next day, the next month, or the next year would have in store for us.

None of us admitted to even knowing anyone from the North except for the teachers at school. But we knew they were our enemy, and that they were going to invade our area soon. We also knew that we were not willing to stand idly by and let that happen.

I personally could not imagine what it would be like to actually shoot someone, or have someone shoot at me. I didn't share that with the others. None of them indicated any uneasiness on their part either. I chose not to think about that aspect of joining up. I chose instead to dream about wearing a uniform and riding gallantly off over the horizon and into the future with my fellow horsemen.

If anyone besides me was nervous about going to war, they certainly weren't willing to show it to the others. I, for one, was pretty unsure myself. What was I getting into? Would I ever return to Churchville? Was this the right move for James Hanger? Perhaps I should have stayed in school. I certainly liked school. I had plans. Going to war had not originally been in those plans.

All those thoughts lingered within me, but I did not share them out loud. What good would that have done? I didn't want to be thought of as dragging my feet or being less enthusiastic than the others. Or, worse than that, having the others think I was a coward.

At camp each evening around the fire, we drank coffee and ate some meager rations we had brought along. Excitement was building as we got closer to our unit. I doubt if anyone slept that last night at all. We couldn't wait to be soldiers.

# Chapter 4
## Arriving at Philippi

June 1, 1861

We arrived at Philippi, Virginia in the late afternoon of June 1. Someone early on welcomed us at a small encampment near a long covered bridge.

I recall our instructions quite vividly. We were ordered to be ready to move at a moment's notice. We were to stay close to those already in camp. The signing of our enlistment papers would have to wait because those officials had already left town.

I found it exciting to watch the soldiers as they drilled and trained. I was anxious to be a part of them. Around the evening campfire, I was all ears, wanting to soak in as much information as I could.

The Churchville Cavalry was nowhere to be found. Later I was told they had been sent to nearby Buckhannon, but were expected to return that evening. When they did finally return, my two brothers, Henry and George, were quite surprised to see me.

June 2, 1861

I spent another day just watching. Everyone was too busy getting our boys ready for a possible federal raid to take time for small details such as getting the new recruits uniforms, muskets, and accoutrements. They shooed us away, telling us to come back another day.

I hung around my brother, Henry, and the soldiers from home. Henry was mighty happy to see me there. But he said my brother, George, was not pleased that I had abandoned mother at home. Henry suggested that I avoid George at all costs if I knew what was good for me.

I was not going to try to buck George. But I did feel like I could fit in with the other boys of the Churchville Cavalry.

About dark, we were notified that we would not move until midnight. Not long after that, it began to rain really hard. At midnight, our move was postponed again, perhaps on account of the rain.

Our officers told us that the federals were moving closer and would be here soon. The Union army was said to be entirely too strong for our forces equipped as we were, having not a single cartridge in the command, only loose powder, ball and shot. And the men in camp were insufficiently armed with old flintlocks, horse pistols, a few shotguns and colt revolvers. The plan was that we were going to high tail it out of town when we got the first inkling of the federal troops approaching the town bridge.

The new recruits were sent to the place the Churchville Cavalry was settled. There had not been enough tents to allow for all of the Confederates (about 800, I would say) to be in the camp. The cavalry had set up near the Garrett Johnson barn along the banks of the Tygart River and just a stone's throw from the bridge. Many crowded into the barn to keep dry as the rain pelted down. Normal sentry duty was suspended due to extremely wet conditions.

Thunder and lightning kept me wide awake most of the night. My immediate thoughts, as usual from such loud thunder, were that the gods were angry.

My prayers for the evening, part of my normal routine, asked God to watch over the boys of the Churchville Cavalry.

The soldiers who had been here for several days already warned us of Union troops on Talbott Hill above the town. We were ordered to remain quiet as the hill was within such close proximity of our camp that we didn't want them to hear us and give away our position.

An officer also told us that we might face our first action of the war in the morning. We were to remain in full readiness. I was pretty sure if the rain continued to bombard us in the morning that the new day would only require that those who had powder would try to keep it dry. I was pretty certain that my first action of the war would more than likely be postponed until another day.

June 3, 1861

As the sun came up, a fog had enveloped the area around the barn. The rain had stopped. Many of us went outside and stretched. Several of us sat down around the fire and drank coffee. Private Ben Houseman asked if I was scared. I laughed. We had just arrived. My heart was beating rapidly from excitement, but I hadn't given any thought at all to being scared. This was where I wanted to be, with my friends from back home. This was my choice. I was determined to make the best of it. I told him that he was foolish and didn't know James Hanger if he thought I would be scared.

Not long after, we heard a nearby explosion. I was ordered to return to the barn to calm the horses. Another explosion followed. And then a third one. That was the last thing I remembered.

*Harpers Weekly* newspaper – July 6, 1861 edition
Battle of Philippi

# Chapter 5
## Aftermath of the Action at Philippi

June 8, 1861

When I woke up today, Robert Dunlap, also of the Churchville Cavalry, who had been wounded in the action and who had been with me, filled me in on what had happened. He explained that I had been mostly "out of it" between being conscious and unconscious since the early morning hours of June 3.

He said an errant cannon ball had bounced off a tree and into the barn, striking me in the leg. According to Robert, I laid for four hours injured in the hay, bleeding profusely. He stayed and tried to stop the bleeding.

Finally Union soldiers came by looking to forage whatever they could find. They found us. And lucky for us, they summoned help.

He said those soldiers rolled me onto a door they had torn from the wall of the barn. They brought back a doctor. The doctor cut my leg off as I lay on the door. Then they treated Robert.

I was shocked to learn that I had been out for so long and was now without a leg. It was too much for me to comprehend at the moment. I was in too much pain to think much of anything though I was curious.

I asked where we were now. He said after the operation, they had carried us across the long bridge and into the United Methodist Episcopal Church. I looked around. Yes, I was pretty sure, even in my pain that I was in a church.

Robert said he was doing all right with his wound in his side which he said was just a minor injury. He asked about my status.

I certainly was not doing well at all. The pain I was experiencing was excruciating. It ranked right up there amongst the most awful feelings I have ever had multiplied by about a hundred. I passed those thoughts on to him.

Robert told me that most of the others in the church were Union boys. He said there were about a dozen of them. I wondered if Union doctors would even look at me. I was the enemy.

Even with Robert's explanation, I certainly hadn't known what had hit me. I had absolutely no recollection of the event that brought me to this church. I don't remember seeing a cannon ball headed toward me or anything that may have happened afterwards.

I lay in the church that had recently been turned into a hospital for what seemed like a very long time. A pretty lass about my age brought me drinks several times and wiped away the sweat from my face. Her touch on my skin was comforting. She said she was from Philippi and was helping in any way she could. Her dress was torn and spotted with blood. She told me that she would mention to the doctor that he needed to attend to me soon. She asked if she could pray with me. We prayed together. I was thinking her request to pray with me was an indication, perhaps, that I was mortally wounded.

She didn't say it, but when she left, I started thinking that this just might be my last day on earth. I tried to find comfort somewhere in that thought, but could find none at all. I did not want to die. I needed to fight with all my resolve to stay alive. I dared not close my eyes for fear that they would never open again. I prayed and prayed that God would spare me. I promised to do better if I were spared. I tried to bargain for my very existence like I had never done before.

I tried to think good thoughts particularly about the pretty girl who had helped me. And I wondered what my mother would think if I were to return to Churchville in a pine box. Would she blame herself for letting me go?

If my leg didn't hurt so much, I would have actually found the situation to be comical. I lay here dying in a Godforsaken little town in the middle of nowhere after spending less than two days in the war. Some cavalry soldier I had become. I had not been allowed to sign my papers and enlist. I hadn't even climbed on board a horse. I hadn't even received my uniform. I had seen not even one enemy soldier. I had not even been issued a musket. I wasn't in a line of fire. Yet I was already a war casualty. How could this have happened so fast? I was embarrassed to have already gone down. This all had to be a terribly bad dream.

I was too young to die. I had thought I would have plenty of time to leave my mark on the world, even though I had no idea what that mark was to be. I had to fight with every ounce of energy I could muster to make it through.

I began to see the pretty young local girl as an angel sent by God. It dawned on me that I did not even know her name. I promised myself to ask her if she returned.

Thinking about what I needed to do to survive was way too much for me to figure out today. But it was a huge concern. And a new concern that I had never had to deal with before.

The lass finally did return. She urged me to hang on. She thought the doctor would be tending to me soon. I asked her name. She said her name was Deborah.

I asked her to get me some paper and pencil. It didn't take her too long to accomplish that task. Even with that, I was not sure what I was going to write or why I thought it was important.

I made the mistake of also asking her if she thought I would make it back home alive. She didn't answer. Instead she started crying and ran off. That was the second time today I had the dreaded thought that pushed everything in my little brain aside and took over. I was thinking that this just might be James Hanger's last day.

A distinguished looking man who appeared quite exhausted approached. He wore a bloodied apron. "I'm Doctor James Robison, surgeon of the 16th Ohio Volunteer Infantry. What is your name, son?"

"James also, sir. James Hanger of the Churchville Cavalry."

"Well, James, I needed to take off your injured leg. Hopefully that operation will save your life."

He poked around. I screamed out in pain. He wiped his now bloodied hand on his apron and approached me again. "It was bad, son," the doctor explained. "Your leg was mangled. That's why I had to cut it off. You did not speak kindly during the surgery about me, which I understand. It must have hurt like hell. You had lost too much blood for me to use an anesthetic."

"I don't remember anything, but it still hurts like hell," I responded. "However, in spite of what I might have said at the time, I am eternally grateful for your work. I definitely do not want to die."

"Hanger, if I had not operated on you, you would not be alive this morning," Dr. Robison admitted. "I sawed your left leg off about seven inches above your knee. You may not survive very long anyway, but your chances are better with an amputation than without one. To be truthful, young man, I am a trained surgeon who has done many operations before. This is not even my first war. I was active in the Mexican War. I have studied and read about how a leg amputation should be conducted. That barn would not have been my choice of locations. But I did have the proper instruments. I want you to know that this was the first amputation I have ever attempted. I also wanted to assure you that if Dr. James Robison didn't do your operation to the best of his ability, there isn't anyone who could have. I worked on you as if you were my own son. Nothing distracted me. You got the finest surgery available. That said, I cannot promise a good result."

"I trust that you did a good job, sir. I know this is going to turn out well. And even if I die, please know that I am grateful that you were my doctor."

The doctor gave me something to drink he said would help me sleep. After Dr. Robison left, I was puzzled because my left foot itched. I looked under the cover and found that impossible. I didn't have a left foot or any part of my leg from the middle of my thigh and below. I was in terrible pain. But what was the use of complaining?

Deborah was waiting when I awoke. I was still lying on a church pew. She said I had been out for several hours. She asked me how I felt. I told her "great" but I didn't feel great. I didn't even feel good. I was feeling miles less than good. I was felling darn right miserable with a capital M.

As the day progressed, the pain was so bad that I couldn't think straight. I tried to pray. I am not sure the words got put together in any semblance of prayer, but I am thinking if there was truly a God in heaven, he would be smart enough to know that I was in need of some of his utmost attention. I thought of my mother and how she would be tending to me if she had been here. I feared closing my eyes.

Deborah brought me something to drink that was pretty strong and surely was not water. She said it was doctor's orders. I was not going to go against the doctor's wishes on this particular day. I had to fight against the pain and the thoughts that it might actually be better if I died than having to endure all this.

Perhaps Deborah could sneak in a gun for me and I could put myself out of my misery. I certainly was no longer any use to the Churchville Cavalry. I was no use to the Confederacy. I had done nothing to aid the cause. I surely didn't feel like that patriot Mr. Walker had talked about at the picnic the day the cavalry left town.

Deborah returned and asked me if I would mind if she said some prayers with me. I encouraged her, thinking that two people praying for my survival was much better than just one.

My thoughts turned to what tomorrow might bring, if I indeed got the privilege of seeing tomorrow. What would I do now with my life? How could this one-legged man make his mark on the world?

I realized that worrying was not productive. I knew too that positive thoughts and visualizing my recovery rather than concentrating on my woes would help me greatly.

I prayed fervently that I would live to see another day.

JAMES DICKEY ROBISON, M. D.

# Chapter 6
## Convalescing in Philippi

June 11, 1861

Deborah said I had been in and out of sleep for three full days. The doctor had told her to keep waking me up periodically to make sure I was conscious. And to have me take some liquid medication that I was to have four times each day. I had not remembered waking up at all.

This day seemed a wee bit better than the last one. After all, I was not going to have any body parts removed today. Actually that was about the only good thing I could think of right now.

Deborah brought me broth. I was starving. I devoured it quickly. She went back and got more. And then went back again.

On a scale of one to one hundred, often used in our engineering classes in school, this day was a few points better than the last one I remembered. Oddly my missing foot still itched. I was not able to reasonably determine why that was. The pain was either lessening a wee bit or I was more tolerant than the day before. I decided to call my first post-amputation day as zero and compare from there. Today was a four.

I was able to look around and better assess the situation. I was lying on a pew in a church. I thought that was a good place for me under these extreme circumstances because I am thinking God would easily be able to find me here. And if he wanted to take me, I was already at the church.

Several of the other boys on the other church benches were noisy, crying out and begging for help. At least I seemed in better shape than a couple of them. Deborah focused on three soldiers near me, while several other ladies cared for the others.

A man approached and asked to speak to me. He introduced himself as Reverend Hindman. He said he was pastor of the church that had become the local hospital.

He thanked me for serving to protect Virginia from the wrath of the invading federals. He asked if he could pray for me. I encouraged his prayer, thinking that it was going to take more than just my prayers to survive the mess I was in. We prayed together. And he left me with this Bible passage on a piece of paper "Verily, verily I say unto you. Whatsoever you shall ask in my name, I will do it." I found his visit comforting.

Deborah brought me a loaf of bread that was still hot. She said the ladies of the town were providing the food.

Dr. Robison checked on me several times. I claimed I was alright, thinking positively, but I was certainly not that sure I actually was. I did thank him again for his work. And thanked God that I was still breathing and alive, at least on some level.

Certainly I was not the same lad who had left Churchville, Virginia just a short time ago. Whatever dreams I had last week, certainly weren't going to pan out as planned. I would have to move on to alternate dreams and plans.

The pain did not allow me to focus very well on anything as important as the future that my life might have in store. I surely would be sent home, as I would be unable to be a soldier. I was not sure that was really such a bad thing. I had changed my mind in thinking this war was going to be glamorous and exciting. What I saw in every direction inside this church made into a hospital was a far cry from anything that I could have ever imagined. There was nothing glamorous or exciting within my view.

As the day progressed, Deborah brought me a full supper. The beef and potatoes were the best I had ever had, or so it seemed at the time. Perhaps I was just a wee bit hungry.

I asked Deborah if any other boys in the church had amputations. She said just one. She said the others were suffering from bullet wounds, with at least one probably having a mortal injury

I tried to sit up by myself, but didn't have the strength to finish the job. I asked Deborah to help when she returned, but she said that was not going to happen – doctor's orders. I was to keep still and rest up.

At the end of the day, I praised God silently for letting me still be breathing and mostly still alive.

# Chapter 7
## Help from Dr. New

June 12, 1861

As the pain started to wane just a wee bit, I took my first long look at what was the remaining portion above where my leg had been. It was raw to the touch. It looked like Dr. Robison had cut a flap of skin and folded it over where the bone had been cut through. There was a hole in the skin. Some kind of cream had been rubbed all over the part that remained. It was ugly, for sure. It was still bleeding through the wrappings that Deborah had to constantly check.

Deborah caught me looking and scolded me. "Ain't none of your business what's going on with your leg," she insisted. Rather than fighting her on the subject, I held my tongue. I kind of thought I had a right to know. After all, it had been my leg or at least part of where my leg had been. And what was left of it was still mine. Long after there was no more Deborah to care for me, I would have to deal with it. I did, however, ask her what the hole was for in the side of the part of the leg that I still had. She said that was to drain the fluid that would build up in the wound.

She brought scrapple with maple syrup for breakfast. I washed it down with whatever Deborah had offered before, that drink the doctor had ordered; the one that was certainly not water.

I looked for Deborah later in the day, but didn't see her. When she returned in the evening, it didn't seem like she was still angry with me from the incident where she scolded me. She brought bean soup which I found

make the stump harden. He said he would visit me while I recuperated here and would continue to tend my injury.

When Dr. New left, Reverend Hindman visited again. We prayed together. He asked if there was anything else he could do. I asked to be moved to a more comfortable pew. He said he was sorry, but that the church benches were purposely uncomfortable so that the parishioners wouldn't dose off during his sermons. While that made sense to me, it didn't make my stay very comfortable.

As Deborah was wiping my face today, I wondered out loud if she liked this kind of work or was just trying to make the best of a bad situation. I told her that she was quite good at providing care. She smiled. She said that she might like to become a nurse. If this war went on for any length of time, I was sure her skills would be in great need. We prayed together again today. My prayer was both in thanksgiving for being alive and in hopefulness that I would see tomorrow.

Using my sliding scale of determining my progress, I would say today was a six or seven. Not good and certainly not great. But it had been a bit better than yesterday. Besides, the goal for the day was to survive. So far I had reached my goal again.

Dr. George Washington New, 7th Indiana Infantry
Indiana State Medical Association, 1891

27

# Chapter 8
## Another Day in the Church Hospital

June 13, 1861

Today I woke and determined pretty quickly that I was still alive and still hurting. I wondered if the pain would ever totally go away. I wanted to sit up on the church bench. Deborah tried to help pull me up. I was not able to help myself. I didn't have any strength. That would have to come another day.

The bench was not the most comfortable place I had ever been on, but I was not complaining. I had to keep reminding myself that my main goal was to survive. I prayed and kept positive thoughts in my mind toward that target.

Breakfast was a large slab of bacon and several eggs. It tasted great.

Several of the town's people visited today. Mr. Morrall and his mother, Mrs. Harper, a lady of probably 80 years old, brought me freshly baked bread and an apple. The bread was still warm and delicious. I told her I was extremely grateful as I needed to get my strength back. Some home cooking was just what this one-legged soldier needed. The apple tasted delightfully delicious too.

When Dr. Robison came by this morning I asked him something that had been on my mind. "Dr. Robison. Why did a Yankee doctor take such good care of this rebel lad?"

He laughed. "Have you ever heard of the Hippocratic Oath?"

I shook my head, admitting that I had not.

"I took an oath to provide as much professional medical help as possible to my patients. There was no designation that I am aware of in my oath that said I should only treat my friends or federal soldiers. You were a patient. It was my responsibility to help you by providing the best medical aid I had at my disposal."

"I find that amazing," I responded. "And I will be eternally grateful, sir." With that I gave him a little salute.

With each passing day it has become more apparent that I was indeed going to make it. I may not be able to do some of the things I had done easily before, but James Hanger was not going to pass by the chance to still make something out of his life.

Reverend Hindman made his daily visit to the wounded inhabitants of his fine church. I was pleased that he allowed me to pray with him again. He mentioned that I seemed to be doing a tad better than the last few days. I agreed, but also insisted that I might still need God's help in making more progress.

I was basically starving and wondering where Deborah was. When she finally showed up, she made a fuss saying she was sorry that she had brought supper so late. She had to run home to help her mother. Supper was worth the wait. It was beef stew and carrots. And as per usual, the pot was large enough to provide me a second helping.

On the engineering scale of success, today was my first day in double figures. I gave the day an 11. I thanked God for the progress but reminded Him politely that I was in great need of His continued help in the days to come.

And while an 11 certainly was the best since my accident, it was not where I wanted or needed to be.

# Chapter 9
## My Missing Foot Was Still Itching

June 15, 1861

As always, my first act of gratitude for the day was to congratulate myself and thank God that I woke up and found myself still alive. I surely was not alive and well, just yet, but I was working on that too. I certainly was eating better and able to sleep more soundly with each passing day and night. The pain was about the same. I wondered if I was going to have to live my entire life having immense pain. And my missing foot was still itching like crazy.

Cadet Daingerfield was being moved today to another location. The boys carrying his gurney made a side trip to pass by where I was. We talked for several minutes. He seemed much more defeated with his condition than I did. We wished each other well as he was carried outside the church.

My thoughts wandered, perhaps due to the medication they had been providing in my drinks. I thought of how angry my mother was going to be when she found out that her son had lost a leg. I thought of Washington College and how my handicap would interfere with an engineering career. And I pondered ways of making my missing foot stop itching. Of the three, the last seemed the least likely to be easily resolved.

I was able to sit up today, with the help of Deborah who was quickly becoming my second favorite person in

Philippi. The first, of course, was Dr. Robison. Deborah and I prayed together. I also thanked her profusely for her fine care. She told me I was only allowed to sit up for a few minutes. She came back before I was able to look around much and helped me lie back down. "Doctor's orders," she said with a smile.

Deborah brought a large breakfast containing flap jacks and sausage, both swimming in maple syrup. If nothing else, I was getting stronger due to nourishment that was almost as good as home. Deborah had more time to spend with me since some of the other wounded soldiers had been moved out. She shared with me that she had overheard officials saying I would be taken soon to a local home to further recover. She asked again if she could pray with me. I found that a comforting part of my day. We also read from a worn Bible she had brought from home.

I started to look at Deborah differently, as in the eyes of someone who I might have been courting back in Churchville. But just as quickly I dismissed the thought. After all, who in their right mind would want to marry a one-legged man?

Reverend Hindman had to wake me up when he visited today. He laughed and said he didn't think the hard benches were conducive to sleep, so I must have been very worn out. I asked for him to pray with me as we had done each day since my arrival. His words to the Lord once again blessed my day and encouraged my survival.

I started thinking about the things I wasn't going to be able to do when I got back home: dance, run, play hide and seek, or even make it from one college classroom to the next without being late. I started getting depressed at the thoughts. I decided instead to make a list of the things I still would be able to do. I was surprised how long that list was.

One of today's Bible readings was "Be Not Afraid." I thought it interesting that Deborah chose that particular passage to read. That message resonated well with me. I rated today at 14. It was another day that I was grateful that I was progressing slowly toward my main goal – survival.

# Chapter 10
## Moving into a Private Residence in Town

June 17, 1861

Early this morning I was prepared to be moved to the home of Mr. and Mrs. William McClaskey in town.

The good pastor, Rev. Hindman, wished me well and said a prayer for my continued recovery. I thanked him for providing his church as a hospital and for his prayers.

Deborah asked if we could pray together one final time. I agreed. She hugged me like a long lost friend as the boys lifted me from the pew onto a stretcher. Her eyes filled with tears as she wished me well. I thanked her for her care, her prayers, and her friendship as I knew I would not see her again. I thought of her as an angel sent by God to get me through. As is often the case, people come into our lives for a specific reason and then leave. I had appreciated her greatly and would always hang onto good thoughts of her.

I was carried to a wagon and taken a short distance through town to the home of the McClaskey family. I was carried to an upstairs bedroom. When I got situated, the family introduced themselves.

William was about 40 years old. He said he and his wife, Catherine, his father and their seven daughters lived in the house. I was encouraged to become a temporary part of the family. Mr. McClaskey explained that he was the Barbour County Sheriff. He said they had offered to help take care of a rebel soldier as a contribution to the cause.

I was introduced to four of their daughters. The other three were visiting their aunt for a couple of days. I wrote down their names and ages. I would have never remembered them otherwise. Their daughters who were home this day were Mattie, 17; Senna, 13; Rebecca, 11; and Rachel, 9.

Mrs. McClaskey and her children provided abundant and good food within minutes of my arrival and placement in bed. They promised more.

I ate it as if it were my first meal. It was not so much that. But it was at least as good as the food brought in by the ladies of Philippi and served at the church. The next thing I knew I was waking up. The bed had been quite comfortable. I must have been worn out from the trip from the church hospital to their home.

As the day went by, I watched the family as they doted on me. Every few minutes one of the girls would ask if I needed anything.

Mattie, the oldest, seemed to be in charge of the McClaskey brood. She ruled with an iron fist, at least when her mother wasn't looking. I saw her bossing the others around unmercifully. I didn't think it was such a bad thing, as everyone seemed to be pretty much in line.

Finally, after hours of constant bombardment, Mrs. McClaskey warned her daughters to leave me alone because I needed rest in order to get well. But they snuck peaks through the slightly opened door as often as they could. If I could have charged five cents a peak, I could have made a few bucks that first day.

This day was quite an improvement over all the previous ones. I would score today at a 19. I now had a very comfortable bed and food similar to what my mother would have prepared. And even though I was missing the aid of Deborah, a constant flow of visitors brought comfort to this rebel lad. Admittedly, I was still wracked with pain. And as you probably guessed by now, that darn missing foot continued to itch.

Sheriff McClaskey stopped by after I had settled in. He said the area was crawling with federal soldiers who had chased the rebels out of town. He hoped that they would leave me alone as I convalesced. Being in the county sheriff's presence gave me some solace in that regard. I am assuming, since he was sheriff, that he was certainly armed and dangerous.

As I lay in pain, I thought of how losing a leg had now complicated my life from here on out. That was assuming that I actually lived, which wasn't a given at this point at all, even though Dr. Robison's report had certainly given me hope.

I had given nary a thought when I left for war that losing a leg was a possibility. In fact, if I had thought about every possibility that existed for James Hanger, losing a leg would surely have not even made the list. When I decided to enlist, I certainly did not think of the possibility of getting killed either. But I probably had subconsciously buried that thought along the way so I would not have to ever deal with it.

At least if I had died, there would be no time to think of what might have been. I am lucky in that regard.

So now what would I do? What was my mother going to say? Would I ever be able to carry on by myself again? I had taken the fact that I had two good legs for granted all my life. Up to now, I could run and jump and do most anything other boys could do. That had all changed. What good was a one-legged man? Would anyone want to marry me? Would I be able to have children? Or would I have to live at home until I died an old man?

It was too much to deal with at this point. Instead, I chose to block it all out and put those unanswered questions away for another day. That again was assuming a lot -- that I even had another day.

Dr. New found me. He dropped off a bottle of medicine with instructions to take some four times each day. He checked my stump and said he was pleased with my progress so far, but that I still was not out of the woods. With the fine accommodations, it certainly felt like I was definitely out of the woods. But I knew what he was saying.

The day topped the engineering scale at 23.

My evening prayer was again of gratitude, that so far the Heavenly Father had allowed James Hanger one more day to live.

# Chapter 11
## Suffering a Setback

June 18, 1861

Day two at the McClaskey's did not go as I might have planned. My stump had started to bleed. That was the one thing the doctor had warned me against. I was embarrassed for getting blood on Mrs. McClaskey's fine sheets. I yelled out for help. Mrs. McClaskey came running. She sent Mattie out to find Dr. New.

The expression "two steps forward and one step back" came to mind. Only in my case it would have been two hops forward and one hop back. I thought I had been doing so well. I was not ready for a setback.

Dr. New came quickly to my aid. When he looked at my bad leg, he said somehow I had knocked part of the scab off, which led to bleeding. He said it was not serious but I needed to be more careful. He rubbed more salve on the stump and bandaged it up. He said eventually the remaining stump should get rock hard.

The doctor said he had inquired about getting me an artificial leg. He said his supply list included peg legs but he had been unable to locate them in the supply wagon.

He told me to take it easy. I asked if there would be a time soon when I could stand up and see if I could balance on one leg. Dr. New said he thought I would be able to do that soon.

I didn't feel much like eating at breakfast. When one of the girls returned to take my tray, she must have noticed that I hadn't eaten much. It wasn't long before her mother came upstairs and lectured me on the need for me to build up my strength.

I knew she was right. My mother would have said the exact same thing. I was just having difficulties with the setback. I wanted to push ahead every day. I didn't want to regress. That word wasn't even in my vocabulary. It was not an acceptable option.

The early part of my day was spent fussing with myself. I felt like I might need to stand in the corner as punishment. Instead, I lay in a fine bed feeling sorry for myself. I let that happen for about an hour. And then I picked myself back up, determined to move ahead, forgetting that anything bad had happened earlier in the day.

Mattie brought a tray with supper. It had a cup of coffee and supper on fine china. The plate was piled high with ham, green beans and sweet potatoes and a dinner roll with jelly. The tray included a note from my hostess telling me to finish my supper and clean my plate or there would be no dessert. Someone took that chapter from my mother's book too. Mattie told me to tell her if I needed anything more and when I was finished with supper.

I did finish everything and was rewarded with a piece of blueberry pie. It was delicious.

Mrs. McClaskey told me that evening she found it peculiar, but several of her daughters expressed that they were afraid of seeing me with only one leg. I promised to keep the door closed and only try to stand up when I was alone. The thought did get me to thinking. Will people be less likely to want to be around me because I only have one leg? I would have to wait for that answer down the road.

All in all, I scored this day at 15, a few points lower than yesterday. It was also my first day that I had fallen back. I was also hoping it was my last day of regression. I did not have time to take even one hop back in my push to get better.

As I got ready for bed, I again thanked the good Lord that I was still alive. I was not angry at Him for today's setback. I was angry at myself. But I was past that now and not giving it any more thought. Everything else would have to wait for another day.

# Chapter 12
## Moving to Cherry Hill

June 19, 1861

After staying just two days, the Union army decided to commandeer the McClaskey house as their headquarters. I thought they had made an excellent choice. But that also meant they were sending me somewhere else.

My farewell to the McClaskey family was about as short as my stay. Mr. and Mrs. and the elder Mr. McClaskey wished me well. The four girls lined up and stood behind their parents just watching. I thanked them for their fine hospitality. I told them I would certainly miss the great food, the comfortable bed and the four little smiling faces of their daughters.

I was carried out of their house and placed onto a wagon. I was moved, this time to the home of Thomas Hite that was known as Cherry Hill.

Mr. Hite was a farmer with seven children. His large farm was just north of the town of Philippi. Mr. Hite explained that he and his wife, Evaline, had allowed their buildings to be used as a hospital. Six other injured soldiers were being cared for somewhere else on the farm.

I was helped by the father and a son to a fine upstairs bedroom, even nicer than the one I had just vacated in town. I was hoping that the food would be comparable too. When I got settled, Mrs. Hite asked me if she could introduce her family to me by marching them into my room. I said I would be delighted to meet them.

She brought them by, lined them up, and proudly introduced them to me, one-by-one. Again, I took notes so I would remember their names. There were three girls, Mary D, age 18, Henrietta, age 11, and Mary V, age 10. There were four boys, but their older sons, John, age 21, and William, age 17, were both away in the war. Those remaining home included Thomas, age 15 and Samuel, age 6.

As Mrs. McClaskey had done, Mrs. Hite ordered the children to stay out of my room and leave me alone. She said I would not get better if they were bothering me.

When the food arrived later, I had a really hard time deciding which food was better, the food at the McClaskey house or the food being served here. It was really a toss-up. And I knew I was in good hands again from the fine folks of Philippi.

Just as he had assured me, Dr. New visited not too long after I arrived and redressed the wound. He said the bleeding had stopped for now. And that was good. He also surprised me by delivering a wooden peg leg. Actually it was hardly a "leg". In fact, it was just a peg. He said it was designed to fit over my stump and to actually allow me to stand and remain fairly well balanced.

I laughed out loud. Dr. New asked me why I was laughing. I told him "Mr. Hite is going to be very angry that you sawed off a leg of one of his fine tables for this." Dr. New laughed too.

"No sirree," Dr. New assured me. "This is no ordinary table leg. This is actually an official government issued peg leg. No table has been desecrated or diminished in order that you were able to receive this leg. I think you will find it adequate."

I laughed again. "A Yankee leg no doubt," I replied, thinking to myself that *no Yankee leg was going to suit this Virginian.* He laughed again, shaking his head up and down, agreeing with my assessment of the origin of the "leg".

He helped me attach the peg leg tightly. He helped me get up. Dr. New even walked next to me for support. He encouraged me to practice walking. He showed me how to take the peg leg back off.

At first glance, you might have said "it is a miracle. James Hanger can walk." But I was not really walking. I was shuffling along slowly and hoping the peg leg would follow along. The leg was remarkably loud. It made a clunk on the wooden floor with every other step. I was afraid I would scratch the bedroom floor. The peg leg was also quite uncomfortable. And it was not quite long enough for a man of my stature.

The good doctor left as I was in the midst of practicing my walking. He said he would check in on me again tomorrow.

No deference or disrespect to Dr. New, who I had actually thanked for his attention and for delivering the peg leg. But I certainly did not find the peg leg "adequate" at all. Besides being loud, I found it annoying, as it slipped and had to be readjusted about every other step. I found it mostly useless, although it did provide for some support and allowed me to balance.

The procedure of having to take the peg leg off before bed felt demeaning to me. And I knew I was going to have to strap it back on again in the morning. But I guess, in the big picture, a Yankee peg leg was better than nothing. It was just not a whole lot better than nothing.

I could not imagine living my whole life with a peg leg. It might have been alright if I had been a pirate. But I was no pirate. I was determined to accept a peg leg only as a very unsatisfactory and quite temporary alternative until I could determine how to find something better to take its place.

When the day was over, I rated my first day at the Thomas Hite home as a 24, which was a new high. Admittedly though, the pain persisted. I thanked God for my new comfortable location, for allowing me to still be alive and even for the dang Yankee leg that was now in my possession.

Cherry Hill – Thomas Hite residence
Building was torn down in the 1950s
Photograph courtesy of Noel Clemmer

# Chapter 13
## Trying Out the New Peg Leg

June 20, 1861

When my hearty breakfast was finished, I strapped on the peg leg and started practicing again. I walked back and forth across the bedroom, trying to be as quiet as possible with my new peg leg. But I feared the noise downstairs would bring someone running to find out what was happening.

Mr. Hite stopped by and talked to me. He commented briefly on my new peg leg. He said he noticed I now had two legs again. I was grumpy and probably disrespectful in saying that what Dr. New had given me could hardly be defined as a "leg". And I shared that at first I had thought the good doctor had sawed it off from one of Mr. Hite's fine tables. Mr. Hite found that quite funny. I laughed with him.

When I looked up just after Mr. Hite had left, the door had been pushed open and little Samuel was staring at me. I motioned for him to come in.

He said, "I ain't supposed to bother you."

"Come on in, lad," I said, signaling for him to get closer. He looked around for his mother. Not seeing her, he snuck in and closed the door behind him. I motioned for him to come close. His eyes were focused directly on my peg leg. Of course, to be fair, that was just about straight ahead in his normal vision. He reached out and touched it.

"I lost my leg in the war. This is my new leg. How do you like it, Samuel?"

He shook his head back and forth. "I not like it. Do you?" he said, loud and clear.

"Me neither. In fact, I hate it. I am going to take it off." It was too late. He had already fled the room, shutting the door behind him.

I am thinking that the idea of my being able to take my leg off did not appeal to my new friend at all. I was sorry to have made the suggestion. I filed that in my brain for future reference. In the future I should not announce to anyone that I was going to take off my leg.

In my struggles with my new peg leg, I refused to score myself better than the previous day. But it wasn't any worse either. I scored it a wash and listed the day as a 24 for the second day in a row. Even so, I still thanked God for the opportunity to have lived one more day. I assured Him that I would be even more grateful for another one tomorrow.

# Chapter 14
## Looking for Samuel

June 21, 1861

Today at the Hite house I started by strapping the peg leg on and practiced walking around the bedroom. I peeked out the door looking for little Samuel. He was nowhere to be found. I asked his oldest sister, Mary D, when she brought in breakfast where Samuel was.

"He was real upset about something yesterday," she explained. "No one was quite sure why. But he said he wanted us to go outside and look for something he thinks you lost."

I was puzzled. Then it dawned on me. I had specifically said I had lost my leg in the war. And Samuel was trying to find it for me so I didn't have to wear my peg leg. I explained that to Mary D. She thought it made sense. But we were also puzzled as to how I could explain that to a little boy and get him to understand.

Dr. New returned. He asked me how I was getting along on two legs. "Two legs," I said loudly. "I don't have two legs. I have one real leg that God gave me at birth and one genuine Yankee table leg that you brought to me yesterday. Only one works. Only one is useful. Only one bends at the knee and functions at the ankle. How would you like to wear this piece of furniture on the end of your thigh?"

I didn't wait for him to answer. I reached down and took the darn thing off and threw it at him. Fortunately, I am a really bad shot. The peg leg went tumbling across the floor, coming to rest against the far wall. I hopped over to the bed and sat down. I looked at the doctor.

"I had that coming," Dr. New explained. "I am sorry. You are right. This is a pretty sad substitute for your God given appendage."

The room got quiet. There was a knock on the door. It was my little friend, Samuel. I motioned to him that he could come in. He looked down the hallway for his mother. Not seeing her, he entered and closed the door behind him. He jumped up and sat by me on the bed. His eyes this time went straight to my stump.

"Your leg still lost?" he asked.

I told the doctor what had happened. And that Samuel had been looking for my lost leg. And then I tried to carefully explain the situation in the language that a six year old might understand.

"I didn't really lose my leg. That was just an expression. I am sorry that you didn't understand what happened. I was injured by a cannon ball. Doctors had to cut my leg off. I will never have two good legs like you have."

He moved slightly further away on the bed. His eyes were still looking at my stump.

"Did it hurt?" he wanted to know. I think he was actually beginning to understand.

"Yes, Samuel. It hurt something fierce. And it still hurts. And it will probably hurt for a long time."

He moved closer and laid his head on my arm, right above my stump. His little hand reached out to touch it. I let him. I didn't want him to be afraid of me or my stump.

Dr. New asked if it was all right to remove the bandages and put more medication on the stump now. I asked Samuel if he cared to watch. He shook his head no, jumped down from the bed, and quickly fled the room, shutting the door behind him.

"You are good with children," Dr. New said. "I hope someday you have some of your own."

He treated my stump and re-bandaged it. There had been no new bleeding.

When Dr. New left, I laid on the bed thinking about my experience just now with Samuel and with what the good doctor had said. And that maybe I would marry and have children after all. After today, I was certainly going to consider that a possibility.

When I went to bed tonight, I rated the day as a 30. It had been a very good day. I had been blessed by God to have this day and reminded him before I went to sleep that James Hanger was very grateful.

# Chapter 15
## Another Day with the Hite Family

June 25, 1861

My day started off well because there was no evidence that my stump had been bleeding. And then I had to hop all the way across the room because my peg leg that I had thrown at Dr. New was still lying near the far wall.

The pain at my stump persisted. I was not sure that would ever go away. It was tolerable; nothing more and nothing less. I was willing to have pain if I was allowed to live. That, to me, seemed like a good trade-off.

It didn't take a genius to figure out that my dismemberment would affect me every single day of my life as I moved forward.

Today there was more good food. And more practicing with the peg leg that was a poor substitute for the real thing. And another sneak visit from my new friend, Samuel. When he came in today, I was sitting on the bed with my peg leg strapped on.

I stood up and walked from the bed to the door and back. His eyes followed my peg leg.

I stopped and shifted the leg around a bit. I turned around and started to make the same trip again. As I turned at the door to return, the leg slipped and I fell. Samuel ran over and asked "Are you alright?"

I said "Yes. I'm like a little baby, Samuel. I have to learn to walk all over again. I don't think it is going to be easy. I am sure I will fall some more."

When I pulled myself up, I walked back to the bed and sat down. Samuel looked at me and spoke as I had known him to do – right to the point.

"You leaving soon?" he asked. I was not sure, but knew my time was ticking away. As long as I was feeling stronger, I was going to be leaving. I did not know when. But I didn't want to mislead him either. I shook my head yes.

His head waggled back and forth. "No. Don't go." He started to cry, but caught himself. Someone had probably told him boys don't cry. Instead he came close, touching my peg leg, and then quickly left the room.

My little friend was not going to be happy when the news came down that James Hanger, his new friend, was going to be taken from him. That thought made me sad too. But I knew I had to move on.

The pain was the same today. I needed to remember to ask Dr. New if I was going to have less pain anytime soon.

I am counting today as a new high. The score was 37. I was grateful to God and to Dr. Robison that so far, was so good. I was still alive and apparently doing at least as well as could be expected. And I prayed that when I finally got home, my mother would be accepting of my new condition.

# Chapter 16
## Bad News Arrives

June 26, 1861

Today Dr. New visited and brought bad news. I was being moved again. Not only was I leaving the fine accommodations and hospitality of the Hite family, but now that I was well enough to travel, I was going to be sent to a prisoner of war camp in Ohio.

I had foolishly forgotten that there was a war going on. I had conveniently not remembered that I was a federal prisoner. I guess my stay at two fine Philippi residences had put me in direct denial about the realities of my situation.

As if being without a limb was not bad enough, now I was headed to a federal prison. And although I had absolutely no prior knowledge of prisons of any type, the idea of being a prisoner of war certainly did not have a pleasant connotation.

It was exciting to have the doctor determine that I was making good progress, while at the same time it was not good news as to where I was now going. It seemed like every day was a new surprise. And as long as I was having another day, I was determined to make the best of it.

There had been times recently that living to see another day had not been a guarantee. As of this point, however, I was going to live. And that pretty much trumped anything else I might have to face.

Dr. New checked on my stump and declared it was doing well. I asked him if the pain I was having was ever going to go away.

"That, Mr. Hanger, I am not going to be able to answer," Dr. New explained. "I am not well versed in that area."

I thanked him for his care. I wished him Godspeed. He shook my hand and said he hoped I lived a long life.

The Hite family, right down to their smallest member, Samuel, was not happy that I was leaving. I wasn't either. They had treated me as fine as if I had been their own son.

When it was time to leave, after a nourishing breakfast, I walked carefully and slowly down the stairs on my peg leg, hanging on tightly to the railing. The family was lined up, father, mother, and the children, in chronological order. There was not a dry eye on the female members. The boys showed that they were tough and did not cry. All wished me well. When I got to Samuel, his father intervened. "Samuel has made you a present to remember our family by. With my help, he made it in the nearby blacksmith shop."

I carefully kneeled down on my good leg, trying to get the peg leg out of the way. Samuel reached out his hand, telling me to reach out mine and close my eyes. I closed my eyes and held out my hand. I felt something being placed in my hand.

He said it was alright to open my eyes. There in the palm of my hand was a small metal cross, slightly crooked, and obviously hand made by Samuel with some help from others. I looked him in the eye. "Thank you for this fine gift. Good bye, Samuel, my little friend."

"Please come back again someday," he said, like a lad much older than his years. And then he fled and didn't look back. I hugged his father and mother and thanked them, assuring them that I would indeed come back to visit. I also promised to cherish Samuel's cross for as long as I lived.

By the end of the day, I was lying in a dark train car heading for somewhere in Ohio. Even with my future in doubt, I considered today had been my best day yet. I gave it a 50 score.

As I clutched the little cross, I prayed that the next stop on my journey would be at least tolerable. My goal was to live. So far God had answered that prayer to my satisfaction.

Cross made by Samuel Hite

# Chapter 17
## Welcome to Camp Chase

July 5, 1861

Upon leaving Philippi, I was taken along with several other Confederate soldiers by railroad to somewhere near Columbus, Ohio to a Union prisoner of war camp called Camp Chase. Robert, also from the Churchville Cavalry and wounded at Philippi, was with me. We arrived in the stockade today.

We had the dubious distinction of being the first rebel prisoners to be incarcerated in what we were told had been a recruiting facility for Ohio soldiers fighting for the Union. We were also assured upon our arrival that our stay would not be long, as prisoner exchanges were expected to be occurring soon.

Our first day was mostly learning the ropes of what we could do and what we couldn't do. There were many rules. Among them was not getting close to the "deadline", a line about ten feet inside the wall we could not cross because the guard would shoot us.

We were herded into a shoddy looking shack with places for 18 prisoners in the building. There we were all assigned bunks. I got a lower bunk due to my dismemberment with Robert on the top bunk. There were a dozen similar shacks nearby.

I was tired from my travel by the end of day one at Camp Chase. The day's score had definitely taken a nose dive from the previous day in Philippi. I scored it as a 37.

I took Samuel's cross from my pocket and prayed. It was a prayer of gratitude and hope.

Camp Chase – POW prison near Columbus, Ohio
http://eakycivilwar.blogspot.com

# Chapter 18
## Life in the Prison

July 10, 1861

Today about two dozen civilian secession supporters were herded into the prison at Camp Chase. Several of the men were madder than hornets, already trying to negotiate their way out of jail. Three who were assigned my shack claimed to have been a newspaper editor, a judge, and a sheriff. They were in general of a most pathetic demeanor, begging and whining that "there must be some mistake." They demanded to see the commandant of the prison.

I determined today that there were at least as many rats as prisoners in our shack. I was told they tasted good, but didn't care to try, even if I were real hungry. Body lice were frequent invaders into our clothing and were annoying pests. Robert said we should call them "gray backs". The name stuck.

The food at this camp was definitely worse in both quality and quantity from what I had received recently at the McClaskey and Hite homes. In the shack we had a pot belly stove for cooking. A kitchen sergeant cooked for the men and passed the food through a hole in the wall in a tin cup. Today we each got a potato, a chunk of bacon and a small, stale loaf of bread. And while I wasn't going hungry, I would have eaten more in Philippi if I had known prison was the next stop on my journey.

Coffee was our only reliable staple. With brown sugar added, it was often the only item we consumed that we did not have to question what it contained.

It rained hard today. We set out buckets to collect it as fresh water in the prison was at a premium. The roof leaked so much that we were as wet as if we had been outside of the shack.

Our supper was the combination of navy beans (about a spoonful per man) and a finger-sized portion of some kind of meat. The joke was to identify the food, which was as difficult to identify as it was to chew. I had absolutely no idea what the meat was on this day. One man swore the "mystery meat" tasted like dog. I was not sure how he would have known what dog tasted like.

I talked to a sutler who said he stopped by the camp about once a week. He thought he might be able to find me a crutch that would help me get around. I encouraged him to look. I told him I had money to pay him for his service.

I walked back and forth in the shack several times each day trying to practice walking with my peg leg. It made so much noise it seemed like it might be pretty annoying to all the others. The peg leg was also very uncomfortable. I don't think it had been designed for someone whose amputation was so high up on the hip.

I would have to say today was no better than the last one. It scored my second straight 37 on the engineering scale.

Once again, I held my crooked cross as I said my evening prayers. I blessed Dr. Robison and Dr. New for saving my life. And I thanked the Almighty that James Hanger had been allowed to live another day.

# Chapter 19
## The Sutler Helps Me

July 17, 1861

Today the civilians were all released from the stockade. No one would say what they had actually done to cause their incarceration. If their arrest was intended to shut them up, it hadn't worked. They ran their mouths and complained the whole time they were here. Did they expect the prison to be like a rose garden?

Unfortunately, our stay was much longer as soldiers from the Confederacy.

Each day we were joined by more Confederate prisoners of war. Today our population was probably doubled from when we first arrived here. We were told this morning that if we voluntarily signed papers to fight for the Union, we would be released. Our decision had to be made by 5 o'clock in the afternoon. They got no takers from our shack.

One of my biggest problems at the prison was balance especially when I was at the open latrines. Even with my peg leg, I feared I might lose my balance, fall in, and not be able to get back out. That would certainly have been a horrible way to die.

Each time I got outside, I took the long way around to practice walking. Guards watched my every move from parapets high above the stockade fences. The guards were positioned right above the "deadline".

I doubt if they feared that I would run off, but the guards eyed me suspiciously anyway. They had muskets and sometimes fired into the prison. I was quite fearful that some trigger happy Union guard would take target practice on me, a prey who would have little chance of dodging a bullet.

God bless the sutler. He brought me a crutch today that I am thinking will help me greatly. He asked one and a half dollars. I thought that was a fair bargain. I gladly paid him and thanked him for his efforts.

The crutch was just a little short for me, but I am determined to use it anyway. I am thinking that once I got used to it, it would make it much easier for me to get around. Between the crutch and the peg leg, I would be able to move around most anywhere if I were careful. But truthfully, the peg leg would have been much better suited for knocking out one of the prison rats in preparation for adding him to our next prisoner of war meal.

I found it odd that officials allowed local citizens to pay to tour the prison. Both men and women came through the shacks during the day, mostly gawking at us. Prisoners often were quite ignorant in their comments especially to the ladies, causing several damsels to run out of the building screaming.

As rebel soldiers, we were evidently the new attraction in town. I am not sure that we looked much different than the federal soldiers. I wondered how much the people paid to see us, and if they thought in the end of their tour that they had received their money's worth.

I had bigger worries than the bad food, trigger happy guards, local citizens on tour, rats, lice, or the living conditions. I was trying to survive. That took my attention and prayers twenty four hours a day, every single day.

At first I was greatly troubled by both my present condition and the outlook for my future. Neither was very rosey. But if I didn't survive, I would have no future anyway. It was pretty pointless to worry about tomorrow or the day after or anything beyond that. I had to make it through today. I would worry about tomorrow if and when it arrived.

I was careful to watch the healing on my stump so that it did not get infected. I was concerned with my ability or lack therein of being able to move around with any stability at all with my Yankee peg leg. I thought it better to proceed slowly for the time being even with my new crutch.

Of course, everyone in prison camp wanted to know my story and how I came to have one leg less than any of the rest of them. If I had remembered the actual incident, it would have made for a better story. To tell them I basically did not know what hit me seemed quite inadequate to most of the boys. They all had stories too. I am not sure to what extent they were telling the truth, the whole truth, and nothing but the truth.

Men told of their training which I had obviously missed out on. They talked of what they were trained to do if captured. Their instructions were to give only the necessary information to the enemy which included name, regiment and rank, but nothing else. They said we should expect to be subject to a prisoner exchange within a reasonable time after capture. And that they had an ultimate responsibility to try to escape.

Escaping may have been in their future plans, but I was unlikely to be physically up to running off when the guards weren't looking. I told the other prisoners to not tell me about any of their escape plans, because I did not want to hold them back or drag them down.

The camp medic did come around to check on me every once in a while. He was not Dr. Robison or Dr. New, but I appreciated that he at least looked at my stump and provided some ointment for my wound. He assured me that I would be exchanged soon and would be able to go home to recuperate. While that sounded grand, I was going to cross that bridge only when I got to it.

With the delivery of the crutch today, my day had definitely been improved. Even with the serving of questionable food, the pain that did not go away, my fearful visits to the open latrines, and everything unsavory about this prison, today was rated as a 45. Things were improving in the life of James Hanger.

My prayer tonight as I clutched my tiny crooked cross was to wake up alive tomorrow. It seemed like a simple request. I didn't think it was too much to ask.

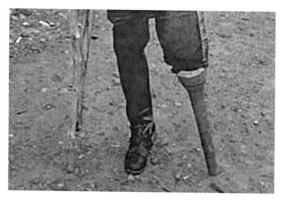

Peg Leg
www.fitnews.com

# Chapter 20
## Waiting to be Exchanged

July 20, 1861

Prisoners' names were called each day for exchange. I waited patiently with anticipation without getting my hopes up. I remembered a Bible phrase that seemed appropriate for the day – "Many are called but few are chosen."

I tried to continue my recuperation by building up my strength and practicing walking on my peg leg. Several other prisoners expressed genuine interest in my new leg and its capabilities. As far as I was concerned, the peg leg had no capabilities. It was just there, allowing me to stand up. And that was it. A peg leg had no other practical use that I could see. It would have been just as helpful if they had left it attached to the Yankee table where I imagined it had come from originally.

The other prisoners were surprised to hear that I had only been in the rebel cavalry for less than two days, and that I hadn't even received a musket, a uniform, or a horse when I was injured. I was getting the reputation of being not only the one-legged man, but the rebel soldier with the least experience prior to my capture. They joked that if the Union officials in the prison interrogated me, they would be quite unlikely to find out any Confederate military secrets.

I was allowed to write a letter and mail it today. I wrote to my mother, telling of my incarceration and potential exchange. And that I would be coming home soon. I didn't want to surprise her. I also told her that I had been wounded, but was recovering nicely, without actually saying that her youngest son was missing a leg. I wanted to break that in slowly. Obviously, it would not take her long to figure that out once I actually arrived at home.

I was not sure how long it would take a letter to reach Churchville, Virginia that would be mailed in Ohio. Perhaps I would even beat the mail delivery home.

The doctor returned today to put more ointment on my stump. There was no apparent bleeding. The hole was allowing for the fluid to drain off. I asked the prison doctor if I could trade my peg leg in for a fancier model, but he didn't see the humor in the situation.

Today was absolutely not one iota better or worse than my previous rating. I scored it as another 45.

Tonight as I prayed, I thought of how grateful I was to be still breathing and taking nourishment. As I rubbed my little cross, I thanked God for today and asked Him if I could be allowed to have another day tomorrow.

# Chapter 21
## Enjoying Irish Stew

July 25, 1861

It was day twenty in the prison. It was a sunny day which made it unbearably hot inside the shacks. The camp was starting to have a stench about it that was very unpleasant too.

Robert and I talked about what it was going to be like to go back to Churchville. I reminded him that he should have an easier time than I was going to have. I told him of the McClaskey girls who were afraid of me because of my missing limb and wondered if the neighbors would have the same reaction.

He said when he recovered from his wounds, he wanted to find the Churchville Cavalry and ride again. That too was easier for him to say. I was pretty sure one-legged cavalry soldiers were pretty scarce in Confederate service.

Today's new menu item was Irish stew, prepared by some local merchant who had donated the items to the prison. It was by far my best meal since leaving Mrs. Hite's cooking.

I continued to fret over my leg pain, which had not lessened at all. I could tolerate it by now, but truly would have rather that it had been non-existent. And darned if my missing foot wasn't still itching. I wondered how it could still be a problem.

Every night when I bedded down, I thanked God that I had made it through another day. I asked for tolerance and understanding from my mother when I got home. I asked the good Lord to bless the Churchville Cavalry. I also had a special prayer for my brothers, Henry and George, rubbing Samuel's crooked medal cross during all those nightly prayers.

Today was another wash as far as progress had gone. No progress. But no regression either. It was another day I rated at 45.

# Chapter 22
## My First Month in Prison

August 4, 1861

Today marked one month since we were delivered into Camp Chase. There was no exchange in sight for either Robert or myself, though several others had been sent home. I hoped and prayed our names would be called soon.

The tally for one month is as follows: one month of all bad meals except for that one "Irish Stew Night"; of worrying about my falling to my death at the open latrines; of slight healing for my stump and practicing with my peg leg; and part of the month having a crutch to lean on. It was also one month of several things I could not have imagined one month ago – being in prison camp, recovering from an amputation, and not having one inkling of what lay beyond the next day in my life. There was also a whole month of days and nights still filled with intense pain.

As you may have figured out by now, I was no happier with my peg leg than I had been on day one. If I were a table with only three legs, I would have been ecstatic about the addition of a fourth leg. But as a man, I was not excited at all about having a peg leg -- especially a Yankee peg leg.

The new leg did allow me some balance while standing. In combination with the crutch, I could certainly move about with greater ease than I could have had I needed to hop from place to place. It was generally better than nothing. But it didn't make me happy.

Robert was as impatient waiting to leave as I was patient to wait. Don't get me wrong. I will be as excited with the announcement that we were going to be exchanged as anyone. I was just not ready to celebrate until we got actual official word. I would cross that bridge when I got the opportunity. Meanwhile, I would make the best of my time as a prisoner of war.

I am thinking there were about 250 prisoners total in camp today. Several had died since our arrival. I believe they all had been ill before coming to the camp but were not helped by what I would deem unsanitary conditions here. They had been taken outside the prison to the hospital and did not return. Soldiers here thought the federal doctors in the hospital would probably not treat a rebel prisoner very well. They were surprised to hear that my amputation had been done by a Union doctor.

There were two main problems of the prison shack: the roof leaked when it rained, and there was absolutely no ventilation. An additional problem came on a hot day like today when the hot weather and the stove worked together to heat the air making staying inside almost unbearable.

Today's rating was a 46. It was no better or no worse than any comparable day in recent memory, but I gave it an extra point because I thought it was good that I have survived the Yankee prison for a whole month.

I continued to pray for survival. Surviving seemed more likely as the days have gone by. As Dr. Robison had told me, if I were going to die, it would have probably happened already. As I held the little crooked cross before I went to sleep, I thanked God that the wayward cannon ball had not taken my life. James Hanger still had things to do.

# Chapter 23
## Our Names Are Called

August 5, 1861

Today was day thirty one of my stay in this prison. Today both Robert and I were notified that we were going to be exchanged. We whooped and hollered like two school children. If we agreed to take the oath, we could return to our homes in Churchville, Virginia.

We took the oath, as follows: "I do hereby solemnly swear that I will bear true allegiance to the United States and support and sustain the Constitution and laws thereof; that I will maintain the national sovereignty paramount to that of all state, county, or confederate powers; that I will discourage and forever oppose secession, rebellion, and the disintegration of the federal union; that I disclaim and denounce all faith and fellowship with the so-called Confederate armies, and pledge my honor, my property, and my life to the sacred performance of this, my solemn oath of allegiance to the government of the United States of America."

I didn't know about the other lads, but with only one good leg to stand on, I was hardly going to take up arms against anyone except maybe if someone entered my home and threatened my family. But I did know this. I was going to give my oath to just about anything they wanted me to promise them that day just to get out of the Camp Chase stockade.

I couldn't speak for Robert. But I had a feeling that he was pledging to go home, but not real serious about discouraging any rebel activities. He was itching to ride again with the Churchville Cavalry.

We were released and taken by wagon to the train station where Robert and I were put on the cars of a train to be shipped to Norfolk, Virginia. It is a good day. Today I scored it as my best so far -- a 55.

I prayed a few minutes before lying down in the train car to sleep. I held my little cross in hand thanking the Lord for delivering me from Camp Chase and putting me on the train to Churchville.

# Chapter 24
## Going Home to Churchville

August 12, 1861

Today Robert and I arrived in Norfolk, Virginia. We were processed and then provided with release papers we could show to anyone who asked. That was important because we didn't want anyone to think we were deserters. They shot deserters.

After we got to Norfolk, we figured we were still about 200 miles from home. We were not alone. Several others were headed in our general direction.

After a lengthy and tiring journey via several wagoneers who probably felt sorry for the one-legged boy hobbling their way on his peg leg and with his crutch, we reached Churchville on the seventh day after leaving the prison. I said goodbye to Robert and wished him well. I was ready to convalesce at home.

As I walked slowly to the house, I wondered what the reaction would be. I negotiated the porch steps and knocked on the door. My sister, Anne Eliza, answered, quite surprised as to who was calling and yelled to the others.

My mother and sisters ran to me. They seemed extremely happy to see me. They hugged me mightily. They cried this time both tears of joy that I was home and more than likely cries of horror that I was missing a limb. It didn't seem like my mother would ever let me go. She whispered that she had been told by a neighbor that I had been killed at Philippi.

I asked if she had received my letter. She had not.

No one at home said a word about my peg leg. I kind of expected that they wouldn't. But I was pretty sure that they had noticed. It was quite obvious that something was amiss about the James E. Hanger who had recently left home to join the cavalry.

My mother doted on me to the point of being almost ridiculous. I wasn't in need of sympathy, just support. I wanted to scream that I was still the same James Hanger who had left not too many weeks earlier and not someone new and different. I bit my tongue. It was better not to say anything.

Mother asked what I needed. I told her what I needed most was plenty of her good food as I wanted first and foremost to regain my strength. Beyond that, I wanted to be left alone.

I was already quite tired of my Yankee peg leg. It was extremely non-functional except to help my upper body with balance. But it really had no other uses.

I had given some thought from the day my Yankee peg leg was attached to me that I wanted to build a new leg to replace it. I envisioned some sort of device I could attach to my stub that would at least provide some stability and functionality. I was not sure what it would have to look like, though I was thinking all along that it would probably be helpful if my new limb in some way resembled the leg I had been born with. After all, that one worked really well when it was part of me.

I am guessing my engineering training at Washington College had something to do with giving me the confidence to imagine that I might be able to build a better leg that would at least be an upgrade from the peg leg.

It was by far my best day since my amputation. Its score was 72.

My prayer tonight was in gratitude of being home. As I held the tiny crooked cross, I wept for some time. I was home. I had survived. It was time to forge some new goals.

Hanger home on Churchville Avenue
where James E. Hanger recuperated in 1861
Home was torn down
It was where Churchville Volunteer Fire Company now stands
*Staunton Leader*, Bicentennial Edition, July 2, 1976

# Chapter 25
## Recuperating at Home

August 27, 1861

Each time they climbed the stairs to bring me a meal, my mother or sisters would find the tray and empty containers from the last meal and a note with the list of supplies I needed. Since arriving, I had asked for a hammer and nails, any type of hinges they could find, wood screws, leather, barrel staves, strips of metal, a saw, a plane, sand paper, and whatever scraps of lumber they could find. Amazing as it may seem, somehow with each wonderful meal, I got more and more excited about building a new leg.

Mother always left some kind of note on the tray. I kept them all. They were short and caring. "Please come down stairs and join us for supper." "The neighbors left you these flowers." "We prayed for you at church this morning." "Everyone in town is worried about you." "Your brother Henry wrote and asked about your well-being." "Robert Dunlap stopped and wanted to know how you were doing." "Reverend Arnold said his parishioners were praying for you."

My mother always knocked when she left the tray. She never entered. She spoke loudly saying the same thing each and every time. "Your food is ready, James. I have brought the other supplies that I have been able to find. I hope you are feeling better." My response was the same too. "Thank you, Mother. I appreciate everything." And I certainly did.

The only time I left my room was to make trips to the outhouse. I was not as quiet as I wanted to be in struggling down the stairs as my peg leg and my crutch made lots of noise. The first few times the whole family arrived to watch by the time I was halfway down the stairs. After a while, they started ignoring the routine and left me alone.

The home cooking was helping me regain my strength. The supplies were quite valuable as I set out very determined to find a way to give myself the two legs that God had provided me with upon entry onto the earth, or at least some semblance of same. That had become my new goal.

I knew that whatever I constructed was not going to be as good as God's leg. But I also knew that anything I could build had to be a far cry from only having just one leg or from having a Yankee peg leg. Somewhere in the middle is where I was heading. That direction became my passion and my challenge. It consumed all my thoughts every single day.

At first, absolutely nothing I tried worked at all. I was frustrated and angry. Originally I admit being angry with God for putting me in this awful position. The more I thought about it, I lessened that anger and realized that this situation might not be all bad.

I was angry too that even as a fairly competent workman, I was dealing with devices and situations that were beyond my capabilities. I also knew that I had the rest of my life to solve the problem. I wasn't going anywhere. I certainly did not need to be in any hurry at all. And I could give up at any time along the way and just have one good leg.

But if you knew James Hanger, you would already know there was no giving up in me. In fact, the angrier I got at the situation, the more determined I became. I dreamed of having two legs. I believed I would have two legs. I knew I would have two legs. There were no ifs, ands, or buts about it. Nothing was going to stop me. I just had to stop being in a hurry. Time certainly was on my side.

Dr. Robison had warned me against bleeding. None had occurred since that one time at the McClaskey's house. I thought that was encouraging.

The doctor had also told me lots of people with amputations would not live long afterwards. But he didn't know James Hanger. That being said, I was very careful to keep an eye on the wound each and every day. I watched it so that I could determine if anything in the color or texture of the wound changed. I was immediately on top of any and all progress or lack therein. Actually, I thought the way Dr. Robison had handled the amputation probably was a blessing for me. And as Dr. New had projected, the skin at the sight of the wound was hardening. He admittedly had not known if my leg would continue to be painful. It still hurt terribly.

I am thinking that most of the war surgeons had little or no experience in the surgery they performed. But fortunately for me, Dr. Robison had read some articles on the subject and had come prepared. I was blessed that this Union surgeon even took time for me, a rebel lad, when he had others from his own army to treat. And I was doubly blessed that he believed in the Hippocratic Oath and didn't withhold medical attention from me even though I was the enemy. I guess that is just one of those extra blessings God gave me, along with the misfortune of being in line of that darn cannon ball to begin with.

Oh, if I had only stayed home like a good little lad. That would have made mother happy. But no, I had to do my part. Some part I had. I had barely arrived. I was in a barn, not out in the front lines with the others. Some dang Union artillery soldier was so bad of a shot that he hit a tree near the barn instead of where any of the enemy may have been. He missed everything in sight.

Yet the cannon ball took the unlikeliest of bounces and hit me in the leg while I was inside the barn. It was a terrible shot for sure. He would have flunked his artillery class with a shot that far off target. I doubt that he even knew he hit anything at all. He probably forgot about that shot because it was so far off whatever target he was aiming at.

And it was just plain dumb bad luck on my part. It was utter coincidence that I was the soldier who was at exactly the wrong place, on the wrong day, at the wrong time, and somehow in direct line with a cannon ball that had no idea where it was heading. If I believed in coincidence, I would have thought this was the day the stars had lined up against me. No matter what I did, I was going to be in the direct line of that wayward shot.

For some reason, I am beginning to think James Hanger might have actually been chosen to be hit by that cannon ball. Though I am not sure I will ever know why.

As I stayed as a recluse in my room, my thoughts went back to the barn where Dr. Robison operated on me and my recuperation in Philippi, Virginia. I thought *I cannot look back on those days without a shudder. No one can know what such a loss means unless he has suffered a similar catastrophe. In a twinkling of an eye, life's fondest hopes seemed dead. I was a prey to despair. What could the world hold for a maimed, crippled man?*

Today I abandoned my recovery rating system. I was pleased at my progress. I was totally sure of my survival. And I had better things to do with my time.

As I did every single night, I prayed tonight holding Samuel's crude little crooked cross. I asked God's forgiveness that I felt anger toward Him for the situation I was in. And thanked Him profusely for allowing me the ability to survive. I asked another favor. Could He please help me to figure out how to build a replacement leg?

# Chapter 26
## Continuing My Work

September 18, 1861

I cannot imagine what my mother and sisters thought I was doing in my room. They had to have heard the banging of the hammer, the sawing of the lumber, and other noises emanating from my second floor bedroom. For some reason, I saw no need to tell them. I was alone, in my own world, trying to deal with the loss of a leg while at the same time gaining my strength and inventing some kind of new-fangled artificial leg.

I remembered that a man who lived in Churchville had a peg leg too. I didn't even know his name. I remember reading the book "Treasure Island". The pirate had a peg leg. And that was alright for the man in Churchville and the pirate. For some reason, deep down inside, I wanted something more. Something I had not ever seen but could visualize. Something that worked like a leg and just wasn't an item you would find in the corner holding up a table.

I felt the need to talk to the local man with the peg leg. I wanted to hear what he thought about his loss. I filed that away as something I needed to do when I was able to get outside and walk into town. I am thinking it would be helpful to compare notes with him.

I studied my good leg from top to bottom, trying to figure out how it worked. I flexed it back and forth. I tried to determine the angle that my ankle would bend, side to side and up and down. I studied my knee joint. I needed my new leg to be similar in capabilities to my good leg.

My new leg was going to have to bend at the ankle and at the knee, just like my natural leg. It would have to have an ankle that could flex from side to side, turn back and forth and be sturdy enough so it would not come apart when I put all my weight on it and tried to move about.

I drew pictures of the joints, starting with my good leg. I imagined what my good leg might look like without the skin. I tried to figure out how the joints were held together and how they operated smoothly and efficiently. I laughed thinking that a mere man, James Hanger, was really, for all practical purposes, trying to duplicate a fine piece of machinery most ably concocted by God. It seemed an impossible and daunting task for sure.

I used the barrel staves I had requested, carving them to give my new leg some shape. I was trying to make it look like a real leg. I used rubber and hinges and springs. Nothing seemed to work. It was a frustrating exercise. I was also as determined as anyone could be.

In a sense, all I really wanted to do was duplicate God's work, which I realized was pretty much out of my realm of possibility. I knew wanting to do something and actually being successful at it were often miles apart. It was difficult for any man to tackle the idea of duplicating with wood what God had developed with muscles and bones. I also knew from experience, that if I could visualize something, I could make it happen.

At times I kind of wished Dr. Robison would have left the amputated part of my leg with me. Then I could have skinned it down and figured out the layout of the ligaments and tendons myself. That information would have been invaluable.

Instead, I sent a message to mother asking one of my neighbors to kill a squirrel for me and bring the carcass upstairs. I know mother probably was as troubled as ever with my request, but came through like she usually did, the next morning. I am thinking she probably thought I was having Mr. Squirrel for lunch as I have had before. But no, this time I had more important tasks for the recently deceased critter. I was going to find out how its leg worked as best that I could. And instead of skinning down my old amputated leg, I skinned out Mr. Squirrel's leg.

I knew full well that Mr. Squirrel's leg was not exactly the same as my leg, but I knew his could not have been that different either. The lesson in squirrel anatomy was actually quite helpful.

From the anatomy lesson, I determined that the operation of the ankle was much more of a challenge than the knee. The knee basically is much like a door hinge, opening and closing. The ankle, on the other hand, was much more complicated.

Besides supporting the foot and being able to withstand all my body weight (which at this point was rising from the good food mother was preparing), the ankle had to twist and rotate laterally. It also had to work in conjunction with a wooden foot.

The ankle joint was at least ten or so times more perplexing to me than the knee joint. I was sure it would also take me many more failures to get closer to the answer I needed.

The foot was the least of my worries. All I had to do was make a wooden foot that looked like my good foot. I could then put a sock on it, put a shoe on it and tie the laces. The only challenge there would be was in attaching it to the ankle and making sure that the ankle was still flexible at the connection.

My thigh presented additional challenges. How would I attach the new leg to my stump? It needed to be a tight fit without rubbing and irritating my stump. It would be extremely painful if it were to aggravate the area where the skin flap was located. The connection also had to be sturdy and not roll around from walking. I had to somehow be able to easily attach it in the morning and just as easily take it back off at the end of the day.

I made drawing after drawing, trying mightily to figure everything out on any particular day. I was in a hurry to accomplish my goal. And then I would laugh at myself, realizing once again that I had time, from now until the end of my life, to perfect this. I certainly had no cause to hurry.

I whittled daily on the oak whiskey barrel staves using a penknife. About every other day I placed a bucket full of wood shavings outside my door so that they could be dumped outside.

I struggled mightily from day to day. The pain only subsided slightly as the days went by. Strangely, my missing foot continued to itch. I never did quite understand that phenomenon. How could a part of my body that was not there keep sending signals to my little brain? It was no longer attached. It was not possible.

If I looked at my stump once, I looked at it a hundred times a day. It was important that I was able to remember its exact measurements. My continued worry was how to attach my new limb securely. If it wasn't attached properly, it would come loose at inconvenient times. And I would be picking myself off the ground more than I might have liked.

This may sound odd, but I missed my lost leg. I even think I mourned my loss. I felt it on some days. Perhaps I was losing my mind. I didn't know if this was normal behavior for someone who has lost a limb. It was something I needed to ask the man with the peg leg.

As always, my day ended in prayer. Tonight I prayed that although I was grateful for today, I would like to wake up alive again tomorrow to continue the task that I had been working on.

# Chapter 27
## Returning to the Living

November 14, 1861

When I finally was finished with my project, I walked carefully down the stairs, holding on tightly to the railing. I had purposely left my crutch upstairs. My mother and my sisters seemed totally amazed. Mother hugged me like she thought that I might not ever have come out of the room. My sister, Anne Eliza, on the other hand, clapped loudly. At first I thought she was clapping due to my arrival down the stairs. But her eyes were on my artificial leg. She seemed impressed.

I showed off my new leg for them. I showed them how it attached and how the knee and ankle operated. I was excited that my sister was impressed. That didn't last long. Mother scolded me for making her think I was distraught and maybe even suicidal. I apologized profusely, not intending in any way to mislead her at all. I guess I had been so focused on my project that I did not take her possible thoughts into consideration.

I walked slowly around the house. I had to stop several times to reposition the leg. It was difficult to keep my new wooden foot pointed straight ahead. My new leg was uncomfortable and would take some time to get used to.

Each time I walked, I would note the pros and cons of my experience in my journal. Then I would change something here or there and proceed with a slightly different leg. I was learning as I went. It was trial and error all the way along. That is not always the best way to learn something. But in this case, it was the best way for me under the circumstances.

I had also figured out some other things. I had begun to realize that the cannon ball and the amputation had changed the direction of my life. I didn't see the two events as being a disaster any more. I was starting to see that good might come out of this after all.

I had also become aware that for all my life I had taken things for granted, like having two good legs; having a loving family; and being able to see, hear, and think.

I promised my mother that henceforth I would join them for all meals and any other family activities.

Supper on this day was the first time I had joined my family since I had come home. My sister declared that I had returned to the living. And at least for this meal, it seemed that I was being treated as well as I had been even before going off to war. The fact I was missing a leg, for the first time, seemed not to matter to anyone in my house.

I knew others with only one leg, regardless of how they lost their leg, must have had some of the same thoughts I had been having. Did they also have a damaged sense of their former self? Were they wondering if they could carry on with their lives? Were they fearful what others might think when they saw them? Would people notice our missing leg first and make judgment before they really got to know us?

I was pretty certain it would be important that those of us paddling along in this same "one-legged" boat needed to compare notes and lean on each other for support.

As I unhooked my new limb and started getting ready for bed, I prayed as usual. Tonight I prayed with much gratitude for "returning to the living" as my sister had suggested. And I asked God to prepare me for the multitude of challenges that still were ahead for James Hanger.

# Chapter 28
## Walking Around Churchville

November 30, 1861

As I felt stronger and practiced walking on my new leg, I ventured out of the house. At first, I was truly walking alone. Although the neighbors watched from their windows and porches, none actually ventured out to greet me.

As people observed me from afar, I observed them. At first I thought they were curious. Perhaps some saw me as some kind of "freak of nature". Perhaps I could get a job with P.T. Barnum and be a sideshow billed as "The Man with the Amazing Wooden Leg." The thought annoyed me a bit. But I was also sure that as soon as the novelty of the sight of a man with an artificial leg wore off, they would come out and talk to me. It only took a couple of days.

My neighbors Calvin and Joann Brown were the first to approach and talk to me. They had known me for a long time. They were certainly as curious as the rest. But they had talked to my mother. She had told them that I was doing well. They called out and invited me into their house for some tea.

The conversation was war-related at first. They wondered how long the darn war would continue. Many originally had not thought it would go on as long as it already had. I wondered that myself. I was surprised that it was continuing daily. Mr. Brown said he had read that the Confederates got a recent victory at Manassas Junction.

Eventually the leg became the focus of both the discussion and the attention. I rolled up my pant leg and showed my new artificial leg proudly as I would have presented a treasured item at the "show and tell" segment in my early school days. I described what I had done to provide a hinge at the knee and movement at the ankle. I explained how I had been frustrated with the Yankee peg leg the doctor had fitted me with. And that I was trying to build something better.

Calvin asked if it hurt. At first I thought he was kidding. I wanted to scream out *They cut my leg off with no anesthetic. Did it hurt? Oh my God. It was the most pain I had experienced by far in my short life. I screamed for hours. I cried. I want to die.*

Instead I told my neighbors that it was a terrible struggle that I wish I had not had to go through. I explained it hurt worse than anything else I had ever experienced in my life. And that I still endured severe pain every single day. I also insisted that I truly believe what doesn't kill me will make me stronger.

I also explained to them that it was important to me and others that the artificial leg was not something I wanted people to notice first when they met me.

Mrs. Brown asked how my mother was dealing with me and my loss. I told her that mother was not doing as well as I was. "My mother thinks that I am not the same person who left to go to war. While I understand her view, I am having trouble convincing her that I am exactly the same person. And like any mother would, she worries about my future because I am maimed. To me, my missing leg is not a handicap but an opportunity."

It was very comfortable for me to speak openly about the situation with Mr. and Mrs. Brown. And all the while it dawned on me that this was going to be a regular part of my day from here on out – explaining to anyone who would take the time to listen as to how my new leg worked.

I was also fairly sure those explanations would help me too. They would help me to figure out as I went along some things I hadn't yet considered. So these kinds of adventures would be basically learning experiences on both ends.

As time went by, I was certain I would be greeted more enthusiastically by friends and neighbors around Churchville.

December 7, 1861

I walked around Churchville for the exercise. It also gave me the opportunity to get the feel of how the leg worked and how I might make it function better. I walked slowly, testing the new leg while at the same time not wanting to put too much stress on it and have it break.

As the days passed, I got braver and ventured out further. I needed to have my new leg get lots of work. I wanted to check with each and every application to see if my new limb would hold up.

Several times I fell. Each time I documented why I thought I fell. I wanted to know if it had anything to do with the construction of the new leg. That way I could make small changes to the apparatus to try to overcome the problem.

Early on I noticed that once my knee bent, it didn't automatically go back into its neutral position. That presented another challenge.

The attachment of my new wooden foot and ankle were still not functioning properly, at least to my satisfaction. The foot needed to flex more, and the ankle hinge needed to have the strength to lift up the foot.

Each trip outside the house was a new experience. And with each jaunt, I documented what was good and what was not so good about my new limb.

I was quite aware that leg #1 was just a beginning. I was determined to continue to build new models and test them out.

It wasn't like I was building something and asking someone else to test it. I was testing it myself. Since I was my own critic, I would not settle for anything less than the best. No one could make a leg that would be as good as the one I could make. I don't mean that to be boastful. I mean that in the sense that I would certainly know best as to what I needed.

I was learning by doing. I started out having none of the answers at all. Someday I hope I would be able to look back and laugh at the simplicity of that first attempt. I would certainly find it laughable as to how utterly useless it will be compared to the new and improved models that follow.

After a while, people stopped and talked to me. Even those who hadn't known me before knew that I was James Hanger, the man with the new artificial leg.

I am sure they were curious about me. But I wasn't foolish enough to think they crossed the street just to meet me. I knew my artificial leg was the big new attraction.

Just like the rebel prisoners were the attraction at Camp Chase, my new leg was the talk of Churchville.

It had not dawned on me that my new leg would be such a topic of conversation. People stopped by the house, not necessarily to see me, but to see the new leg James Hanger had made. If I would have taken it off and left it downstairs, they would have made their visit to the leg and left without ever speaking to me. That seemed laughable to me from the start. I had created a monster. Now what was I going to do?

The man with the peg leg stopped me on the street. I asked his name. He introduced himself as Mike Sutton.

He asked if he could look at the entire leg. I rolled up my pant leg. Mr. Sutton looked the leg up and down. He said without hesitation, "Can you make one of those for me?"

Without even thinking, I said "Of course, I can."

I asked Mr. Sutton to stop by the house soon. I told him we needed to compare notes on what it was like to have only one good leg. He thought that was stellar idea. He said he had never discussed that topic with anyone in his entire life.

I was determined to talk about my new leg and show it off, so that people would comment and question me. I wanted to hear them out. I wanted them to tell me their thoughts. I wanted to express my ideas out loud.

Their thoughts were all over the place, but they were also often quite helpful for me.

Here's a sampling of what I heard. "If God had wanted you to have two good legs, he wouldn't have let the cannon ball hit you." "That leg will last longer than you will." "I am sure that maple wood will work better." "Hanger, you are a genius." "I guess you would do anything to get out of having to be in that darn war." "With your pants over that, I doubt if anyone would know you have a wooden leg." "You might be onto something here, Hanger. I hear there are lots of soldiers who will be coming home from the war missing a leg."

I took notes and listened intently. There was some really good information that had come out of all this. I thought *maybe the result of the ill-fated cannon ball really was an opportunity for James Hanger.*

I made more sketches. I thought and thought about ways to improve on what I had made. Obviously this was my first try. I was sure I could do better. I dreamed of making wooden legs. I can't imagine anyone else my age having those kind of dreams. But I did have those dreams almost every single night.

My mother and my sisters continued to be supportive. They tolerated all the attention from the local folks that was focused on me. Mother talked to several hunters and asked them to round up some pieces of wood on their travels. The hardware store owner showed me a catalog of hinges. He showed me some springs that I might use to bring the knee back into its normal position. There were hundreds of kinds of springs and hinges. I ordered some so I could see what their capabilities would be on my next model.

Visitors continued to find our house to visit with me. Several were from towns miles away who had heard the news. They sought me out to look at my new invention and to see if the artificial limb was as amazing as people were saying it was. Many expressed the thought that it was much more impressive in person, up close, than any description would have been.

If I had thought of it, I could have made a fortune by charging admission to see me and the new leg. P.T. Barnum would certainly have jumped at the idea and toured me around the country in his traveling side show. I would have been famous with the likes of General Tom Thumb and his famous Siamese twins.

A traveling salesman even stopped by one day and asked to speak to me. "Mr. Hanger," he said. "I think you have got yourself something of great practical use. If you can make me some of these wooden legs to take on my rounds, I think I can sell a bunch for you."

I was flattered and just a bit taken back. I was making this leg for me. I was perfecting it for me. Every one that I made would be better than the one before. The purpose with each new leg would be for me to be able to walk better than the time before.

The thought of making wooden legs for others had not been on my mind since Mike Sutton, the local man formerly known only as "the man with the peg leg", suggested the same – that I make one for him.

I thought and thought about it. Was this why the accident happened to me? Am I destined to make wooden legs for others? Does that really sound like a good idea? Can these legs be mass produced? Am I up for such a task?

The more I thought about it, the more the expression from the Bible rang in my head. "Those that have more will be asked to give even more." Yet I had actually been given less. I had one less good leg than the average person. Why would I be asked to give more? The more I tried to push the thought away, the more central it became.

Almost every single day now I was being visited by someone interested in seeing my new leg. As I had thought before, if the leg would have been on a table in the parlor, people would have visited it and never even met James Hanger. But I didn't let that happen. Everywhere James Hanger went, the new leg went with me, attached at all times. And everywhere the leg went, it was attached to James Hanger.

I wore pants down over the leg. I wore a sock and a shoe over the wooden foot. Yes, I had a slight limp. But I am also certain that any stranger I met would have had a hard time believing I was an amputee from the war. I found it amazing too how much confidence the wooden appendage brought back to me. The event at Philippi, Virginia had not broken my spirit as it certainly might have for someone else. In fact, it had made me stronger. That James Hanger lad who had enlisted and ran off to war certainly was not the same James Hanger who was now proudly walking down the streets of Churchville without even the aid of a crutch.

Balance sometimes was a problem. I admit to that. Sometimes I had to hold onto a rail or fence to maintain my stability. Balance was something I wanted to work specifically on in my next wooden leg model. It seemed to me that the problem might be more related to the foot. I needed to make the foot more flexible.

My hinges had to be kept lubricated. I had to keep the wood moist too so it wouldn't crack and break.

Several more times I toppled to the ground. Once my ankle completely locked up. My next step sent me tumbling down a small hill. I am not sure what caused the locking up. Another time I stepped on a rock and twisted the ankle hinge so badly that I had to take it apart when I got back home to replace it.

I also was very sure that what I had built was a hundred times better than that peg leg which was pretty much universally accepted by anyone who was missing a leg.

Maybe that traveling salesman was telling the truth. Maybe James Hanger actually did have something bigger than James Hanger, bigger than Churchville, bigger than Virginia and maybe even bigger than I could imagine.

Tonight my prayer was in gratitude. I was grateful for what I had been able to accomplish so far, and just as thankful for perhaps new possibilities.

# Chapter 29
## Meeting with Mike Sutton

December 12, 1861

Mother and I talked. She knew some good business-men in the area who could offer me some advice. Mother's encouragement was all I needed to reach out and talk to those merchants. With those local men, we started to discuss what might be a business opportunity.

Upon their request, I broke the new leg down into its separate components and put a price on each individual piece. A spring cost so much, a hinge so much, the lumber was this much, and the labor was that much. They asked me to determine how much one leg would cost. And then they helped me to determine how much less I could make each piece if the individual parts were purchased in quantity – say 100 hinges at a time as opposed to just one. They showed me how buying more would actually cost me less per piece.

Today Mike Sutton, the man with the peg leg, stopped by the house and asked to talk to me again. And just as I thought, he doubted anyone in the whole area knew his name. But they did know him as "the man with the peg leg".

"I was born with my right leg only being formed from about three inches above the knee – the rest was always 'a missing'," Mike explained. "As a youngster, I hopped around and got along about as well as anyone. I was fast at that hopping stuff and could play around with the other boys and hold my own."

"When I was at my granddaddy's house one day, he let me pick out anything I wanted in the catalog for my sixth birthday coming up. I picked a peg leg. I was so excited. But when the new leg arrived, it wasn't quite like it was pictured in the catalog. My stump was curved and the head of the peg where it attached didn't match up. The stump and the wooden leg never quite fit. My father worked with the wooden leg in his shop for weeks. I would try it and he would take it back and work on it some more. It never fit right even with all the changes he made," he continued.

"It has been a disappointment for me all these years. I have tried and tried to make it work. I have put a rubber piece on the bottom to quiet it down, 'cause people could hear me coming. It makes lots of noise. I can't tell you how many times it has slipped out from under me or just detached itself on its own. Each time I hit the ground harder than the time before. You would have thought by now I would have learned how to fall without hurting myself. But I have not. The leg is a peg, but it is not a leg. It is misnamed. And on most days it is just plain annoying. It is basically useless. The peg leg is not functional. It is so obvious that when I meet people, their eyes go right to my peg leg. It's like a sign that says 'that's him – the peg legged man.' I think sometimes the next thing they look for after the peg leg is for a parrot on my shoulder or a patch over my eye like the pirates all have."

As I listened, I was empathetic, for sure, remembering that my first artificial leg was also that noisy, non-functional peg leg, similar to Mike's. I explained to him that my thoughts had been the same. What he was saying was certainly ringing true. I was probably the only one he had ever met who knew exactly what he was talking about. I listened intently as he continued.

"Some days I just want to scream. I have threatened to burn my peg leg, saw it into pieces, or simply throw it off the porch. There were days when I would just as soon go back to hopping around like I did years ago. I go for days not even attaching it to my body. It is not part of me. It is not me. It is like having a third eyeball. What use would a third eyeball be unless it was in the back of my head?"

"As for your new leg, Mr. Hanger, it actually looks a lot like a real leg and seems to function like a regular leg would," he continued. "It bends here and there and twists from side to side down at the bottom. It actually has a shoe attached. If I had a leg like that, people who saw me would not know immediately that I was a man with a missing leg. They would have to look closer. Some might even miss it all together and not know I had a deformity, especially if I wore my pants over it."

Mike continued. "I have never had a pair of shoes in my life. If I had a leg like the one you have made, I would be able to have my own first pair of shoes. People might even get to know me as Mike Sutton rather than 'the man with the peg leg'."

When he stopped telling me his story, I told him mine. I, of course, could not relate to having only one good leg at birth because my condition was the result of a recent accident. I did, however, say this to Mike. "I realized what I was attempting to do with my new leg was a further development in the wooden leg concept. Your peg leg was the best leg they had at the time. One size fit all. Take it or leave it. What I am trying to do is figure out a way so that this new leg will be much more functional than the peg leg, though probably not ever as functional as a real leg. And the first thing I want to do now that I have a good working leg for myself is to build one for you."

He interrupted saying that he would gladly pay for the new leg, even if it took him a couple of years of making small payments every month.

I assured him that his new leg was not going to cost anything. It would be my gift to him. "Going through the process," I told him, "will give me practice in perfecting my own leg. It will be part of my research and development. You will need to visit me often and give me input along the way. I will need to have you try it on at various times so I can adapt it to you. In this case, one size does not fit all. Any leg I design is going to be for a particular person. Whether that leg is designed for you or someone else, the process will be the same. I will need to measure your leg and look closely at your stump. I will have to make drawings of the part of your leg I would have to attach your new leg to. Together we will find the best possible solution to your dilemma."

Mike seemed pleased to the hilt. He was like a child opening a present for his birthday.

I told him about my feelings of losing some sense of existence and worthiness, of wondering what others would think, and wondering if I would be able to be useful in life.

Mike said those same thoughts have plagued him his entire life. "I thought it was just me."

"No," I explained. "I am pretty sure that if I were to talk to others who only have one leg, they might have some of those same feelings. I think it comes with the territory."

My biggest challenge with Mike's leg was the part that attached to the stump. His stump was shaped much differently than mine. His stump was also hard from years and years of growth. His skin was rough like a board.

That compared to my stump that had just freshly been cut open. My wound was still healing a little each day. My stump was red and sore to the touch even while it was obviously also hardening. I am even thinking that since my operation, my stump may have actually shrunk a bit. The place of the attachment of my new leg was much more fragile than his was. His situation was different, but I didn't feel like the challenge was beyond my capabilities.

In thinking about Mike's peg leg, I agreed with what he said – that having a peg leg was one step up from having nothing at all. Or that it was "better than nothing." When he was six years old, his option was having a peg leg or not having a peg leg. I imagine those like Mike who didn't have one would want one. And perhaps those who had one already were pretty casual about it. They could wear it if it suited them or not wear it. As Mike said, sometimes he didn't even wear his peg leg.

My idea was that having a limb missing should not be the first thing someone notices about you. They should know your name, like Mike said, without developing a label about someone that concerned their lack of having a leg.

An artificial leg, I am thinking, should not be noticeable at first glance. It should not be the first thing someone noticed about me. In fact, I want to believe that if I were standing in a line of ten other men who all had two good legs except me, the average person could not pick out the man with only one good leg.

I was determined to prove my idea to Mike. I focused on making a new leg for him that virtually would not be noticeable to the average person who met him. And I believed with all my heart that I was capable of doing that. If I could do that for Mike, could I perhaps do that for others who needed that service too? That remained to be seen.

As I thought about those things, it dawned on me that I had actually revealed something to this man I hardly knew and that I had not even admitted to myself. Yet I had actually said it. I had told him that I was basically going to start making artificial legs for not just Mike Sutton, but for anyone who needed one. From that day forth, the idea of providing artificial limbs for others would become my dream, my challenge and my new goal.

Tonight my prayer was in thanksgiving for receiving valuable input from Mike Sutton. With that came the opportunity for me to help him overcome the nickname that had followed him throughout life. I asked the Heavenly Father to guide me in the scary notion that I might start providing artificial legs for others too.

# Chapter 30
## Doing Some Research

January 15, 1862

I went to the Medical College of the University of Virginia this week by train to see if I could find out about any other artificial legs that had been developed further than just the peg leg. Dr. Charles Bell Gibson, Professor of Surgery, who was on staff of the school, pointed me to their extensive research library. I was surprised at how much I found.

I learned the term "prosthesis" comes from the Greeks and means "an artificial device that replaces a missing body part lost through trauma, disease, or congenital condition." I also learned that a prosthesis for a loss above the knee was called "transfemoral" and that ones for losses below the knee were known as "transtibial". Obviously, my artificial leg would now officially be known as a transfemoral prosthesis.

I learned that prosthesis was a noun and that there was a similar adjective, prosthetic, which could be used for instance in the expression "prosthetic limb."

I also found out that my invention wasn't original at all. In fact, a prosthesis of some type went all the way back to Roman and Egyptian days. For instance, Herodotus, a famous Greek historian, wrote around the time of 500 B.C. of a prisoner who supposedly cut off his own foot to escape from captivity and replaced it with a wooden foot – a type of prosthesis.

An artificial limb was invented in 1529 by the French surgeon Ambroise Pare. Dr. Pare also introduced the procedure of amputation into the medical field as a way to save lives. I could relate. My amputation certainly had been a life-saving measure for me.

Fortunately there were drawings on file that I could research and pick up ideas in the development of a future prosthesis.

I discovered that the first American patent on an artificial leg was filed in 1846 by B. Frank Palmer. His invention received acclaim that same year at the National Fair at Washington, D.C. He opened a company the following year in Meredith Bridge, New Hampshire.

I found a book on the subject called "The First Lines of the Theory and Practice of Surgery" written by Samuel Cooper in 1844. Cooper's book was said to have been the primer on how to amputate. Cooper's advice to the surgeon was as follows: "as little of the flesh should be cut away, as possible; but the more bone is removed, the better." I wondered if Dr. Robison's information had come from that book.

The thought occurred to me during my research that if my amputation would have come below my knee, my prosthesis would have been much different. That artificial leg would have not needed a knee joint as mine had, but perhaps might have been an ever harder problem to attach. And I realized that I needed to work on a transtibial prosthesis too in order to help the other men who had amputations below the knee.

As I thought more and more about the situation, I realized that many of the men who returned from the war with a leg missing would more than likely have serious issues besides having only one leg. Those issues would be the ones that I shared with Mike Sutton; fears that they would stay at home the rest of their life and never venture out, thoughts of being a lesser person than they had been before, the propensity of perhaps becoming reclusive, and fearing that they would not be accepted as a productive, functional member of their town.

To me, the prosthesis in many cases would be a man's ticket back to some normalcy in their lives including possibly returning to an occupation. I thought the sooner that could be accomplished for them, the less problem it would be. And that each situation would definitely have to be handled on a case by case basis.

Unlike the peg leg in which case "one size fits all" my artificial leg design needed to take into consideration the man's height, where on the leg the amputation occurred, etc. And that each one would be unique.

My day, as always, ended in prayer. I was thankful tonight that my association with Mike Sutton had not only been successful for him, but had led to expanded horizons and the idea of my helping others.

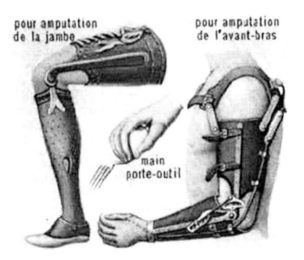

Ambroise Pare prosthesis from the 16th century
www.21stcentech.com

# Chapter 31
## Working on Mike Sutton's New Leg

February 5, 1862

Mike Sutton had visited almost every single day. He wanted to watch the progress I was making. Meanwhile, he was about as excited as any man I had known. He explained that the circumstances offered to him as a man with two legs would completely change his life. A new leg would give him a new sense about himself that would allow him to be more outgoing and to seek to be with people more. It would be much different than his reclusive life that had been his regular routine.

Mike was responsible for dubbing his new limb "the Hanger Limb". I liked that name a lot.

I read in *The Staunton Spectator* recently that the legislature of the state of Alabama appropriated $300,000 for the manufacture and purchase of artificial arms. Their plan called for the purchase of equipment, machinery, and implements to be set up in the state penitentiary to employ convict labor to build the new limbs.

I was both surprised and skeptical. I could not imagine that convicts would have the proper skills needed to make artificial limbs. But I did understand the demand would certainly be there. And that the government of Mississippi probably had it figured out that their convicts would work cheaply.

As my mind returned to Mike Sutton's situation, I thought of those men and boys who were to come back from the war without limbs who might also be homebound for the rest of their lives, too embarrassed to leave their homes and thinking they were less of a man than when they left. That to me would be unacceptable. I thought perhaps there were going to be thousands of one-legged men returning to their homes, on both sides of the war. I saw myself as trying to help every single dismembered veteran, one soldier at a time.

Each day I made progress on Mike's new leg, I wrote down new ideas that frequently popped into my head.

I had to make the foot part more flexible. Just having a wooden foot at the end of a working leg was not acceptable. The foot had to move too. And the toes had to be able to flex as part of the foot.

I continued to try to figure out how to get the knee back to its original place between steps. Right now it was bending the way it should, but not bouncing back.

As I laid down for bed, I picked up that crooked cross and thought about Samuel, my little friend in Philippi. And I prayed that God would guide me on the exciting but frightening path of providing Hanger limbs to the multitudes in the days ahead.

# Chapter 32
## Showing off our Hanger Limbs

February 28, 1862

I finished Mike Sutton's limb within a few weeks. I let him wear it in our house where he could give me immediate feedback. As Mike practiced walking on his newly built leg, he was not shy at all about not liking how the leg felt. And that was a good thing. I needed to hear where the problems were. If he accepted anything less, I wouldn't have been able to make the corrections.

I made small changes and then let him try again. Within a few hours, I let him walk back home with it. He was as pleased as anyone could have been.

For him, the new leg was like another birthday present, but a couple of hundred times better than his 6th birthday gift. His excitement of getting the peg leg in the catalog from his grandfather had been a special time in his life. But for probably 35 or so years, that birthday present hadn't worked out quite as well as that wide-eyed little boy had expected. He had been disappointed many times over the years as the peg leg turned out to be a peg but not necessarily a leg.

Now he was totally ecstatic. I could not have given him anything more valuable than the new leg. It was not so much the leg, but what the leg would enable him to become. His whole life would be changed. He certainly would not be the same Mike Sutton that everyone in the area had known for years as "the man with the peg leg."

I encouraged him to come back and let me know how it was going. I urged him to keep coming back until everything was perfect. And he did.

He returned probably a dozen times to have me make adjustments.

The part that was giving him and me the most problem was the upper attachment, between the new leg and the old stump. I had dug out the interior of the leg so that his stump would fit snugly inside it. Then I tightened it around the outside with laces. When it rubbed him at one place and I smoothed it down, it seemed like it threw it off on the opposite side.

I was patient with him. And he was patient with me. Together we were going to make it work. He thanked me profusely. And then he went on his way.

I didn't hear from him for a while. That to me was as a good sign.

When Mike Sutton's artificial leg was finally finished and acceptable to him, we walked the town's streets together. Now Churchville and the area had two men with artificial legs. Both of us were walking billboards for a future that may include much more functional prosthetic limbs for returning veterans from the war.

My day ended, as per usual, with a prayer before I went to sleep. Tonight my mind went back to Dr. Robison, the Yankee surgeon who had saved my life and made everything to this day possible. To me Dr. Robison was sent by God. Lately I am beginning to see why I was chosen to live another day.

# Chapter 33
## Hanger Limb Factory Opens in Staunton

December 1862

By the end of the year, I had established an artificial leg factory in nearby Staunton, Virginia. Staunton was the largest town in the Upper Shenandoah Valley. It had a population of 4,000 and over eighty businesses including three banks. Mayor Nicholas Trout was a very aggressive businessman, promising me town support and aid in finding employees for my factory. That may have been easier said than done as every able bodied man between the ages of about fifteen and fifty was away at the war. Mr. Trout's status as one of top gentlemen in the county allowed him to connect to both political and economic support for my company.

My customers were mostly Confederate soldiers who had lost a leg in the war, although several were persons who had incurred accidents or amputations that were not war related. One other like Mike Sutton had been born without a leg. No matter the cause, I was more than willing to aid them with their needs.

One of the men I helped was a veteran from Virginia Military Institute in Lexington. I didn't recognize him though I had met him for a few minutes at Philippi, Virginia during my several days convalescing in the Philippi church.

His name was Fauntleroy Daingerfield. He lost his leg to amputation when a bullet hit his knee. He told me his amputation was done in Philippi the day after mine.

I was not surprised to see that he was still walking on a Yankee peg leg. He had been told that his amputation was the second in the entire war. He wondered if I had been told that I was the first. That had not dawned on me at all.

When he visited, I was glad to talk to him. We were "brothers" in the war, two Confederate soldiers who both were injured in the battle on June 3, 1861. The Bath County veteran told me he had been part of Captain A. T. Richards' Unattached Cavalry that fateful day.

I had a similar discussion with Captain Daingerfield that I had had with Mike Sutton. Dangerfield was having second thoughts about his future and his worth. He told me he worried every day what others would now think of him. Like Mike, he thought he was the only one who felt that way. He admitted that he had been reclusive.

I told him that the thoughts seemed to me to be more indicative of the situation. I explained to him that I thought if we talked to many more one-legged veterans, I was pretty certain they would have had the same struggles as we both were having.

He also talked about his missing knee that still hurt. I explained that was happening to me also. It was good to hear that from him, because that phantom feeling in my foot had been an on-going puzzle. And obviously I was not able to have that conversation with Mike Sutton, who was born without his leg. This soldier helped me realize that the itch in my foot was not an indication that I was losing my mind. In the end, Captain Daingerfield was fitted with a Hanger limb.

I wondered if the Churchville Cavalry would have any use of a one-legged man so I could fulfill some of my original commitment for the cause. I wanted to see if there was something I could do to help the Confederacy beyond what my two days of service had provided or rather had not provided. I was able to get myself stationed with the Staunton Home Guard. It did not require much of my attention as the war seemed on most days to be far away from where I lived.

I read recently that the federal government set aside $15,000 to purchase artificial legs. Army Surgeon General William A. Hammond created a committee of surgeons (both civilian and military) to evaluate available prosthetic limbs and approve companies who would provide them. At that time five northern manufacturing companies were approved, including B. Frank Palmer, Douglas Bly, Benjamin Jewett, E. D. Hudson, and William Selpho. Those companies were to provide artificial limbs for Union veterans for $50 each.

I was not sure how they could make limbs that cheaply. Since I had not seen any limbs from those manufacturers, I had to assume that they were not mechanically as complicated as Hanger limbs. I was obviously using more costly materials as I would not have been able to provide anyone with a $50 limb. At the same time, I was excited to know that someone of official capacity was actually thinking about limb loss as being a post war problem.

I also read that the federal government had authorized the formation of the Invalid Corps. It was to be a place for Union men to serve who had been determined to be unfit for ordinary field service due to wounds or disease, but may have been capable of light duty somewhere. These men were divided into two classes – those who were partially disabled but had not used up their term of service from their initial enlistment, and those who had been discharged due to circumstances from the war but still were willing to participate on some level. If, during his duty, the soldier was able, he would be sent back to his original company for duty. Along the way, the units involved had been characterized in several newspaper accounts very cruelly, in my mind, as "the Crippled Brigade".

My thoughts on the Invalid Corps were mixed. While I certainly supported the idea of giving an injured soldier the option to return to some sense of duty, I thought the use of the term "crippled" was not useful. To me that was demeaning and placed a label on someone who did not volunteer to become dismembered.

At the end of the day, I continued to pray for strength and guidance. It seemed like every day I was embarking into new territory. Who would have thought that a wayward cannon ball could have led me on such a challenging adventure?

Hanger Artificial Leg Factory
www.examiner.com

# Chapter 34
## Filing Patents for Hanger Limbs

September 1, 1863

In early 1863, I had filed a patent in Richmond, Virginia with the Confederate States of America Patent Office. The patent, filed with a careful explanation of the working of an artificial leg, included drawings of my latest Hanger limb.

I had learned in engineering class at Washington College of the importance of protecting ideas or inventions by patenting them. I also had been taught that libraries had research on patents that was regularly updated to make sure you didn't try to patent something that had already been invented and was protected. I visited the University of Virginia library prior to filing. That research indicated to me that no one had made anything quite like the artificial leg I was proposing.

I realized that with a patent, I was protected for fourteen years, but could apply for an extension of another seven years if required at the end of that time.

On March 23, 1863, I was notified that my patent, No. 155, for an artificial leg, had been accepted. I was very excited to receive the news

In mid-1863, I filed an additional patent for a newer and better version of my Hanger artificial leg. On August 18 of that same year, I was notified that my second patent had been accepted as patent No. 201.

I knew that the patent didn't guarantee me success on the financial or business front in any sense. It did, however, allow me to proceed without someone else profiting from my ideas and inventions.

As my day ended, my prayer was that the Lord would afford me the opportunity to continue my work to aid those who had similar misfortunes in the long and drawn out war.

# Chapter 35
## Meeting Mr. Lincoln

February 5, 1864

I was surprised to receive a letter today from President Abraham Lincoln inviting me to meet with him at the White House. He wanted to review with me information on the products and services my company was providing. His letter included a pass to allow me to cross from the South to the North and back. My surprise was due to the fact that the Union president would correspond and invite a former Confederate soldier to come to a meeting.

I hired a private coach service to take me to Washington on the designated date, arriving at the White House more than a half an hour prior to my 3 o'clock appointment. I panicked upon arrival, as there was a long line of people waiting to enter. It certainly did not look like I would ever get into the building in time for my scheduled appointment.

Not long after my arrival, a colored man came to the end of the line and asked my name. When I told him I was James Hanger, he told me the president was expecting me. He asked me to follow him. We passed the others who were waiting and went directly into the White House.

I waited perhaps for another thirty minutes. I was finally summoned into an office where I was greeted by Abraham Lincoln. The president was direct in telling me that he did not care which side I had fought for. He had received information from his staff that my company was deeply involved in the prosthetic industry. And he knew that I had lost a limb in the war. He wanted to know more about my company and our products. The president also wanted me to explain how my company was providing this valuable service to Confederate veterans. And he asked me to show him my artificial limb.

I first rolled up my pant leg and showed him the Hanger limb I was wearing. He examined it closely and praised its construction. I explained its functionality and compared it to the peg leg I had been fitted with during the war. I told him of the different needs of dismembered soldiers, depending upon whether their leg had been cut off below the knee or above the knee. And I explained the additional struggles that missing a limb brought into a veteran's life.

I showed him drawings I had brought along for devices designed for below the knee amputations. He seemed interested and listened intently. The president asked a very direct question.

"Mr. Hanger. Are you willing to provide these devices for Union soldiers too?"

I laughed out loud. "I am not being disrespectful sir," I explained. "But it was a Union surgeon who amputated my leg – who saved my life – and who I think about with every other step I take every single day. If I learned one thing in the war, it was from Dr. Robison, my Union surgeon. He taught me that his medical talents were for anyone, regardless of uniform color. My God given inventive skills work the same way. They are for anyone in need – regardless of whether they wore blue or gray colored uniforms."

He congratulated me on that attitude which he called "ecumenical". He said he thought that "if more people had similar thoughts like you and your surgeon, we would have ended this terrible war long ago."

He wondered out loud if the federal government would be willing and able to provide for so many dismembered soldiers. The president told me he was very supportive of those kinds of programs but he was not certain that he could get Congressional support.

I was also assured that when the war ended, Mr. Lincoln would see to it that my company would be included in those government programs. He insisted that he was not interested in punishing my Confederate enlistment. He was most concerned with providing quality limbs to any soldier who needed one.

He encouraged me to continue to develop Hanger limbs. The president even apologized for my injury, as if in some strange way he had some blame.

I thought it quite important that the president was supportive of programs for dismembered veterans. His influence, I was certain, would help get those programs approved.

He said he must get back to talking to those many people who were waiting in line to see him that day. He wished me Godspeed.

As I rode back home and thought about what had happened at the meeting, it was surprising to me that the president was so disheveled. He appeared fragile and distraught, though his handshake was certainly firm. In my opinion, the long war was taking a huge physical toll on this man. He appeared to have been taking the war personally.

My prayer that evening was to bless the president who had reached out to the enemy to do what I would consider being the right thing -- to aid the injured warriors. I asked God that the officials of the Confederacy would somehow embrace the same kind of programs to help our dismembered veterans.

# Chapter 36
## ARMS Provides New Programs

December 1864

While the federal government was proceeding to try to help their dismembered Union veterans, the government of the Confederate States of America was neglectful in offering any services to their veterans who had lost limbs. An association of interested persons, some medical surgeons by profession, established the Association of the Relief of Maimed Soldiers (ARMS) to fill that void in 1864. The organization's primary founder was Charles K. Marshal, a minister from Mississippi. ARMS operated solely from donations and with no funding from the Confederate government. It was run by William A. Carrington, the chief administrator for all general hospitals in the Commonwealth of Virginia.

The object of the new organization was to supply artificial limbs gratuitously to all officers, soldiers, and seamen who had been maimed in the service of the Confederate States. The ARMS charter provided for the organization to furnish veterans such mechanical compensation for lost parts of the human body as may be practicable.

The group identified eight manufacturers in the South who had the capabilities of producing artificial limbs. Those companies were invited to send specimens of their work. They also requested proposals for providing limbs along with projected costs and delivery time.

I corresponded with Mr. Carrington and delivered sample limbs with my proposal. I explained that the legs my company currently manufactured were an improvement on the Palmer limb with the Hanger limb moving the knee hinge back, thereby preventing the leg from flexing backward when weight was placed on it.

Furthermore, I informed Mr. Carrington that the Hanger limbs had overcome early designs that were inefficient and broke down frequently by using rubber bumpers and levers inside the prosthesis. The bumpers and levers helped the new leg, when flexed, bounce back into its original position in readiness of its next step. The rubber bumpers also operated by a compression system that provided less stress on the springs and therefore did not wear out through continual use as was the case in some of my competitors' limbs.

On March 12, 1864, ARMS commissioned my firm (Hanger and Brother Company) to supply artificial legs to any Confederate amputee as one of three approved suppliers. The other two approved were G. W. Wells and Brothers Company of Charlottesville, Virginia and Spooner and Harris. By this time, however, the Spooner and Harris factory was not even in operation.

Mr. Carrington and the ARMS directors seemed destined to provide only peg legs originally. It took lengthy arguments from both Mr. Wells and me on separate occasions to convince them otherwise.

Veterans would be allowed to make their own decision as to which manufacturer to choose. Some, in fact, could even choose peg legs rather than the more functional limbs.

ARMS reported that both Hanger and Wells limbs combined "lightness, strength, and symmetry, were worn with comfort and satisfaction by officers and men in the field and in every station in life, civil and military." At the same time, ARMS estimated that there could be as many as 9,000 Confederate soldiers who might need artificial limbs.

Mr. Carrington received various other proposals to provide artificial limbs. But most of those manufacturing companies more than likely had no idea that producing 1,000 or so legs would not be as easy as it might seem. Manufacturing limbs was different than making gloves or trousers as each limb had to be made to individual specifications. The measurements for each artificial leg depended on many details that most factory owners would not be able to comprehend. Those other proposals were all turned down by the association.

The association required disabled veterans to fill out an application and make an oath before a court official on the truthfulness of their claim.

In my mind, ARMS took rather odd measures under consideration in March 1864 in their attempt to reach their goals. A Union cavalry unit was ambushed near Richmond with their commanding officer, Colonel Ulric Dahlgren, being killed. While Confederate officials were most interested in papers Dahlgren carried that reportedly included a plan to assassinate Confederate President Jefferson Davis, ARMS members sought to look at Dahlgren's body so they could study his Yankee made prosthesis. He had been an amputee with an artificial leg manufactured by S. B. Jewett, a Yankee manufacturer. Mr. Carrington even offered to purchase the body, but settled finally upon purchasing drawings of Dahlgren's leg.

During this year the Confederate government also established an Invalid Corps to allow soldiers who had disabilities due to wounds, amputations, or disease but were still able to serve, to provide some service to the cause.

My contract with ARMS called for me to provide Hanger limbs made of "very light wood enveloped with rawhide which strengthens the wood much more than leather or any other material and then painted or varnished." My company would receive $200 per leg for those prosthetic legs that were at or above the knee and $150 per leg for those below the knee. Two surgeons who lived closest to our Staunton factory, John Charles Martin Merillat and William Hay, were designated as inspectors assigned to our company by ARMS. Their job was to check each leg we manufactured and give it their stamp of approval.

I agreed to provide up to fifteen Hanger legs per month as long as I had enough employees to fill the orders. Employees were scarce. The Confederate government had called all able bodied men into the rebel army. That left slim pickings for possible workers for my factory.

The other impediment to factory production was the scarcity of materials we needed in the factory. Among items scarce for both my factory and the Well's factory included brass, wire, gum elastic, and gum skins.

During the contract, I got several letters from Mr. Carrington criticizing the work from my factory and complaining that the workmanship did not match the samples ARMS had looked at prior to naming my company as an approved supplier.

Actually I welcomed criticism of this kind, because without scrutiny, often we got complacent and sloppy. When I checked, the factory was indeed getting in a hurry to meet the demand. The quality of the work had fallen off. Following careful consideration, the needed adjustments were made, the assembly line was slowed down and the inspectors were asked to be more diligent at their jobs. Those were our last registered complaints.

In 1864, I received information indicating that the Union Invalid Corps, formed in 1862 had been retitled and was henceforth to be known as the Veterans Reserve Corps. They were divided into the First Battalion and Second Battalion. The former was to include soldiers who could still handle a musket and march so they could be used as guard, provost duty, or perhaps parade detail. They were detailed to several Union prison camps at such places as Point Lookout, Maryland; the Old Capitol Prison, Washington, D.C.; and Johnson's Island, Ohio.

The latter battalion was to be made up of soldiers whose disabilities allowed them to be employed as cooks, nurses, or guards at public buildings.

This wasn't the first time disabled men had been used by armies in this country. I remember reading recently that there had been an Invalid Corps in the American Revolution that had been authorized by Congress in 1776 with men missing an arm or leg being assigned to the corps.

In October, 1864, my brother, John, who had been helping me with my artificial limb company, left to enlist in the 5th Virginia Infantry. John was the brother of the Hanger and Brother Company. With his leaving, I found that operating my company became a bit more difficult. Because I was outside the office regularly meeting with veterans and helping them get fitted with Hanger limbs, I had no one to oversee the factory while I was gone. John was only gone about forty days when ARMS arranged to have him detailed back to our company to help fulfill our contract.

About that same time, the *Staunton Spectator* newspaper published a story about me. The newspaper reported, "Mr. Hanger, being possessed of good mechanical ingenuity and too patriotic to be dependent upon the Yankees for an artificial leg, invented by his own genius, and manufactured by his own skill, an artificial leg, by which he is enabled to walk with ease." To date that had probably been the best one sentence description of my legacy. But I was not finished.

In late 1864, our factory operations were suspended for a time due to Union occupation of our portion of the Valley.

At this time the University of Virginia at Charlottesville offered free classes to veterans honorably discharged due to a battle wound. Of the fifty-five students the university had listed on their 1865 roster were twelve who were missing an arm, leg, or foot. And the Young Man Christian Association (YMCA) on campus started providing peg legs to those in need.

I prayed for my ability to keep up with the increasing demand for my company to produce quality limbs for anyone in need. I pray that God would provide answers soon to the impediments for my company including the lack of raw materials and workers.

James Monroe Harris -- recipient of Hanger limb through ARMS
Photo provided by Glenn Land
James Harris is his wife's 2nd Great Grandfather

# Chapter 37
## Complaining about Rising Prices

June 15, 1865

If you would know me, you would realize that I was not a complainer. But sometimes enough is enough. And that precipitated my recent complaint concerning fees we were receiving from the ARMS contract.

As the war dragged on, the prices we were paying for our raw materials skyrocketed. I wrote to Mr. Carrington in January 1865 to try to explain my predicament. I told him that "The cost of material to finish a limb properly in addition to the present cost of the material which the legs are made would amount to much more than we get for them after they are made. We think that if the ARMS could increase our pay in the same ratio with the increased value of specie (or depreciation if necessary) that we would be able to finish our legs as you desire. When our contract was made last spring specie was worth only 10 to 20 dollars (dollars in Confederate notes) to 1 dollar gold – now it is worth from 60 to 80 per 1 dollar gold so that our present pay at present prices of any and everything amounts to almost nothing at all. Material for every kind keeps pace with specie."

When I signed the contract with ARMS in March 1864, a gold dollar was worth $22 in Confederate notes. When I wrote the letter, a gold dollar was worth $50. Several weeks later that same gold dollar was worth $67.

The ARMS' reaction to the problem was to sell $10,000 worth of cotton to England in return for supplies needed for the production of artificial limbs. The trade resulted in making the following items available to ARMS: elastic cloth, brass wire, copper, brass, shoe eyelets, suspender buckles, and the like which were all materials that Mr. Wells and I needed to produce artificial limbs.

The association meanwhile was having serious financial shortcomings. They appealed to the citizens of the South for membership to help pay for artificial limbs for their veterans. Donations came from all over the South. I was surprised and delighted that two donations, one of $500 and another of $200, were made by Confederate General Robert E. Lee. ARMS made him an honorary director for his generosity.

Mr. Carrington suggested that ARMS hire fund raisers to aid their efforts. In our area, the Shenandoah Valley, ARMS hired Reverend Julius L. Stirewalt. In spite of the devastation that the Union army brought to the Valley recently, Rev. Stirewalt was able to secure $35,000 in contributions for the organization.

By January 17, 1865, six hundred and nine artificial limbs were provided to Confederate veterans by ARMS.

On March 11, 1865, the Confederate government passed a proposal from Mr. Carrington to support the ARMS' programs. The legislation called for the government of the Confederacy to provide free transportation to and from the manufacturing site for a veteran to receive their artificial limb, to provide materials at cost that might be needed by the manufacturers, to exempt factory workers from military service, and to exempt all contractors, including the Hanger and Brother Company, from taxation.

However, none of the points in the proposal ever came to fruition due to the simple fact that the Civil War ended with the surrender at Appomattox Courthouse, Virginia on April 9, 1865.

With the end of military action, our factories resumed production. We also had a much larger pool of men who could become possible factory workers as they came home from the war.

According to the records, Hanger and Brother Company had provided 310 artificial legs for ARMS during the year that ARMS was in existence.

In the early part of 1865, I was also pleased to have received an exclusive contract from the Commonwealth of Virginia to provide 1,000 Hanger limbs for Confederate soldiers who could prove residency in Virginia. The work was to be done at my new factory in Richmond.

In order to qualify for approved artificial limbs, the state required veterans to submit an Application for Artificial Limb Commutation stating that they had been a Virginia citizen and that they had become dismembered in the war. They were asked to provide information regarding the assistance they sought and as to when and where their wound had occurred. Their application had to be submitted through their local courts after they had made an oath guaranteeing the claim's authenticity.

The state and federal government programs were well intended but often took months and sometimes years for the veteran to obtain their benefit. That impacted greatly on the individuals and their families. In truth, many disabled veterans found their postwar battles for economic survival, physical mobility, and government assistance programs nearly as difficult to handle as the war itself.

I thanked God now that the war was finally over and that there would be no more dismembered men added to the already overwhelming list. And I prayed that I would be able to continue to keep up with the huge demand for artificial limbs.

# Chapter 38
## The Opening of New Limb Factories

July 1865

I didn't find out until after the war that the federal government had unveiled a program in 1862 called the "Great Civil War Benefaction" to offer prosthetic limbs for disabled veterans. The result, besides providing for the veterans in need, was that a plethora of new businesses quickly organized and opened factories that were designed to make artificial limbs.

Over 200 firms had opened to provide those government contracted limbs which were also funded by the government. Many factories closed down within a short period after they opened. Competition was fierce. Many of the new companies had little regard for quality or service, and in a sense, made the industry look shoddy. It seemed to me quite a few were chasing dollars made available through veteran's programs and had no empathy at all for the dismembered veteran, his needs, and concerns.

It was brought to my attention recently that in Minneapolis alone, a dozen prosthetic limb manufacturing facilities closed within a few years after they opened. While that certainly helped my company, in the long run it hurt the industry.

New companies were always interested in making artificial limbs. A furniture company, for instance, could easily add an artificial limb line to their already established furniture factory. That was the easy part.

Over the years, those new companies failed to take into consideration the affiliated struggles that these veterans had that accompanied their loss of a body part to amputation.

If all a company had to do was manufacture and sell prosthetic limbs that would be one thing. But companies had to be certain the prosthesis fit correctly. If their artificial limb didn't fit, the person wouldn't wear them. Companies had to counsel their customers and teach them how to use their new limb effectively. That often took weeks and months, not just a few minutes. An instructional brochure might be helpful to the veteran, but a piece of paper outlining the company's offerings could not take the place of hours and hours of standing by the veteran and helping him make small strides, virtually one step at a time.

Most companies did not understand that a veteran's stump had to heal before it was ready to receive a prosthesis. And as the stump healed, it often shrunk. If veterans got their stump measured right after their operation, their limb would not fit when the stump got smaller as it healed.

Each artificial leg was only as good as the careful and empathetic employee counselor who supported it. That was why it was important to me that the person who was working with the veteran had to be trusted and believed. In many instances, that was provided by one of my employees who also was a dismembered veteran and who wore a Hanger limb. Those employees were my best advertisements because they had been through the same struggles and doubts that our new customer had been through.

We encouraged each new customer to go slowly. They were told to wear their new appendage for just a few hours the first day and build up slowly to longer periods of time. We encouraged them to take their time and walk carefully. In their excitement of having two legs for the first time in a while, many veterans tried to progress at a pace that was much faster than we would recommend.

We stressed that one of the main problems of any prosthesis was the place of connection between the stump and artificial limb. Sometimes the stump was still sore. Sometimes there was not a good fit and the device had to be re-worked. Other times the artificial limb rubbed against the stump and caused irritation. And every once in a while the man's measurements had been incorrect and we had to take the leg back to the factory and start over.

No matter what the problem was, all of our products were totally guaranteed. We were not finished until the man declared that everything was working to his satisfaction. In some instances that took years rather than days or weeks. That was something the Hanger and Brother Company proudly provided better than any other company.

Our company methods were quite different than most, with our uniqueness most notable in the area of service to the amputees. One competitor, A. A. Marks, passed out cards with instructions for individual veterans to measure their stump and mail their findings to Marks' company with his fee (around $100) in order to obtain an artificial limb.

My policy and procedures included employing men in the field to visit veterans to measure the soldiers' stump at their home. We were not willing to build a limb based on the measurements of someone who could not possibly understand the importance of our complicated method of measuring the area around their stump in order to accept a prosthesis that would fit properly.

Our competition in many areas was no competition at all. And that was why prosthetic companies came and went, while the Hanger and Brother Company maintained and survived.

My prayer on this day was that God allow me to continue on with the challenges and opportunities that were on the horizon.

# Chapter 39
## Our Customers Were All Different

What did my typical customer look like? They only had one thing in common – they were missing a limb, sometimes two. Other than that, they were as different as night and day.

Some were tall and others were short. So they required limbs of different lengths. Their stumps were located in different places on their legs. We had to make one type of limb for the "transfemoral" (above the knee amputation) and a completely different kind of prosthesis for the below the knee amputation or "transtibial".

The veterans we treated tended to be poorer rather than richer, although in almost every single instance, they weren't paying for their prosthesis – the federal or state government was. Our customers were more often privates rather than generals, although we fitted them all.

Our dismembered veteran customers came from the infantry, artillery, cavalry, and even from the navy. At first they were all Confederate veterans. After the war, my customer base changed. There were just as many Union veterans looking for limbs that we manufactured.

And like Dr. Robison, even though my company was not driven by some medical oath, I did not determine to help or not help a veteran based on the color of his war uniform or the color of his skin. I aided them all because I remembered too well that it was a Union surgeon who saved my life.

Here is my tale about a customer that was pretty much representative of most. Wilson Magaha of Charlestown, West Virginia, was a Confederate soldier from the 2$^{nd}$ Virginia. He was wounded, along with many men of both sides, at the battle at Gettysburg in July of 1863. Mr. Magaha's leg was amputated at the lower thigh several weeks after the battle at a hospital in New York. His Hanger limb was provided through the ARMS organization's program.

When I started working with him, Mr. Magaha fussed and fussed. He said at least a dozen times, "I don't want no wooden leg." I was not surprised by his attitude. But each time I was with him, he was able to see my artificial limb, without me having to say a word. I convinced him by showing him rather than by having to change his mind by telling him.

When he finally got fitted for a new Hanger leg and the leg was delivered, he still questioned everything and anything about it. But he also thought I was a genius. I tried not to dissuade him from those latter thoughts.

He fussed and cussed when he had a problem with the device. But I welcomed that. I could not make the customer happy if he did not let us know when there was a problem. We always acted quickly in trying to remedy any problem, big or small, for Mr. Magaha or anyone else.

Mr. Magaha also asked some very poignant questions. I remember one in particular. He wanted to know about the guarantee on his Hanger limb. Our company at the present time had a lifetime, money back guarantee. He asked when he died if his family could get their money back. I laughed at the idea. What was nice about Wilson Magaha was even in his infirmity, he still maintained a sense of humor. I think that helped him adapt better than most.

Another customer, I will not mention his name, was the most stubborn man that I have ever run across. I had to deal with him myself, because no employee in my company could work with him. Nothing ever was right with any leg we ever fit for Mr. X. No matter what we did, we could not please him. His head was harder than his new wooden leg. His demeanor was less flexible than the knee or ankle joints of his Hanger limb. If I had been a lesser man, I would have beaten him over the head until he submitted, using the Hanger limb as a club. But since patience was my strong suit, I eventually wore him down with kindness. After months and months of work, he actually softened to the point of being tearful at a weak moment with praise for what he was able to accomplish with his new Hanger leg.

I continued to ask each dismembered veteran that same question that had puzzled me over the years. Had they noticed any sensation or pain from their missing limb? Many said they too had been bothered occasionally from feelings coming from a limb that had been long since removed. It was not just a foolish notion or my mind playing tricks on me.

For some unknown reason, that "phantom pain" was a pretty common situation. I do not understand why, but the human body seems to remember its wholeness even years after what Mike Sutton would have said when something came up "a missin."

As I prayed tonight I reminded myself that all that I had, including my patience in dealing with dismembered veterans and my engineering ability, had been provided by God. I was eternally grateful.

# Chapter 40
## Officers Who Needed Artificial Limbs

January 1866

Limb loss did not just happen to the line soldiers in each army and navy. There were some important generals on both sides who suffered similar fates.

I read recently that Union General Daniel Sickles had a leg amputated when he got hit by a wayward cannon ball. His amputation was above the knee. Up to that point, our experiences had certainly been similar.

General Sickles was injured at Gettysburg, in July of 1863. His right leg was amputated at the corps hospital in that town before he was transported back to Washington, D.C. His amputation surgeon was certainly not someone who was attempting his first amputation, so General Sickles more than likely had a more experienced doctor treating him. That certainly makes his story different.

Now here's where General Sickles' story became a bit strange. General Sickles heard that the army was collecting "specimens of morbid anatomy together with projectiles and foreign bodies". His response was to donate his newly detached limb in a small coffin-shaped box to the Army Medical Museum in Washington, D. C. The museum had been set up to show the horrors of war and included military medicine and surgical objects. Sickles then proceeded to visit his missing limb on each anniversary of his amputation.

Actually the visitation part is more understandable to me than you might think. I know that people have to mourn the loss of their limbs. I certainly did. But I am not sure I would have visited my leg had I known where it had been buried.

I have received correspondence leading me to believe that General Sickles was fitted with a Palmer prosthesis. Although there are many photographs of General Sickles later in his life, none that I have seen show him with a prosthetic leg. This is my theory, for what it is worth. He may have thought it below him as a retired Civil War general to wear an artificial leg, a device more commonly worn by the soldiers in the lower ranks.

Some soldiers, mostly officers, did indeed choose to exhibit their lost limb as an empty sleeve in their uniform jacket or pants. I have no problem with that whatsoever. Every man has free choice as to how he wants to carry on without his missing limb.

Here's some other information I have gathered. You may know that the famous Confederate General Thomas J. "Stonewall" Jackson had his left arm amputated by his medical director, Dr. Hunter McGuire, just prior to his death. His arm was actually buried near Chancellorsville, Virginia where he was wounded while the rest of his body is buried in the town cemetery in Lexington, Virginia.

Confederate General Richard Stoddard Ewell, who was wounded in the Battle at Groverton, Virginia on August 29, 1861, had his leg amputated just below the knee by the same Dr. McGuire who did General Jackson's amputation. I believe General Ewell was fitted with an artificial leg by G. W. Wells and Brother. Of interest too is that General Ewell returned to action again, only to be shot at Gettysburg on July 3. That time the bullet imbedded in his artificial leg and he was unharmed.

General John Bell Hood, CSA, was hit by two Minie balls at the battle of Chickamauga. His leg was amputated only about four inches from his hip. Hood's condition was so severe that the surgeon who performed the operation sent General Hood's severed leg along in the ambulance thinking that soon he would die and they could be buried together. But General Hood survived the surgery. After the war he had two different prosthetic devices. According to reports, one was manufactured by G. W. Wells and Brother while the other was built by Frederick Gray of London, England. I read that the general preferred the southern made leg as being far superior to the British one. That did not surprise me and in fact, made me smile.

Union General Oliver O. Howard was hit twice in the right arm which was amputated at the battle at Seven Pines, Virginia on June 1, 1862. According to the information I have seen, General Howard did not wear an artificial arm.

The unluckiest officer in the war may have been Confederate Brigadier General Francis T. Nicholls who lost his lower left arm to amputation following the battle of First Winchester. At the battle of Chancellorsville, he was wounded in the left foot requiring another amputation. When he ran for Governor of Louisiana, his campaign asked people to vote for "all that's left of General Nicholls."

I also know of Corporal C. N. Lapham, 1<sup>st</sup> Vermont Cavalry, who had both his legs amputated as a result of the same cannon ball. Lapham, was injured during the retreat of Gettysburg when his unit faced JEB Stuart's

Cavalry near Boonsboro, Maryland. Corporal Lapham's right leg was amputated above the knee and his left leg was amputated at the knee joint by Union surgeon L. P. Woods of the 54th New York Cavalry at a nearby field hospital. Lapham was fitted with two prosthetic devices. He reported later on his status with his new legs saying, "I can walk with ease on level ground, get up and down stairs readily and am getting along much better than I anticipated in so short a time."

Bullets and cannon balls in the war showed no discrimination. They struck whomever was in the path whether general or private, and every rank in between. I prayed that all would be as able to overcome their disability as I had.

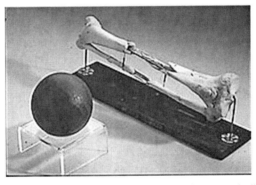

Union General Daniel Sickle's leg and cannon ball
similar to the one that injured him
National Museum of Health and Medicine

Union General Daniel Sickles (center)
at a GAR reunion in Gettysburg, Pennsylvania.
wwew.civilwarny150.org/sickles%20history.htm

"Newspaper Woodcut of General Daniel Sickles
Viewing His Leg at the Army Medical Museum."
(NCP 1727) OHA 250: New Contributed Photographs Collection
Otis Historical Archives
National Museum of Health and Medicine

# Chapter 41
## Negative Attitudes Prevailed

March 1866

I have been gravely concerned with the attitudes of the general society following the war in relation to soldiers who had missing limbs. The federal government seemed to think the proper place for these men was an insane asylum. That was perhaps due to the public anxiety that dismembered veterans needed to be supervised, lest they slip into idleness or something worse.

There was little concern for rehabilitation or deciding that these men might eventually be able to lead useful and productive lives. There was not much thought by others that these men might be able to work at a job and learn to fend for themselves. Instead of support, many attitudes leaned more toward wanting to shun or segregate these victims of the battles.

There were also attitudes coming from some of the thought that "bad things happened to bad people"; therefore anyone who lost a limb during the war probably deserved it for reasons unsavory but obviously also unknown. To many people, the disabled were hopeless but not necessarily harmless and that they might become a burden on society.

Those attitudes were prevalent, though in my mind, shamefully wrong. And those thoughts added to the blatant disregard to the rights of these veterans that not only declared that "all men were created equal" but that everyone in this country was entitled to "life, liberty and the pursuit of happiness."

Organizations were slow to support the soldier who returned home missing a limb or who had multiple missing limbs. I was pleased to hear that the Union League in Philadelphia, Pennsylvania did, however, establish a committee to provide these wounded veterans with employment.

There seemed to be an ingrained prejudice in this country even against the names these legless and armless veterans were called. The terms "invalid", "crippled" and "maimed" were demeaning on almost every level. To me, these veterans had enough personal problems that being dubbed by others as "crippled" just added to their struggles.

During the war, the Union Invalid Corps had been given uniforms significantly different from the established garb of the Union soldier, therein sending the subliminal message that the Invalid Corps was not worthy to be dressed like a regular soldier. Towards the end of the war and following months of criticism, the federal government relented and started to dress their newly named Veterans Reserve Corps soldiers in regular Union uniforms.

Medical curiosities, such as the amputated body parts and photographs of several emaciated skeletons of survivors of Andersonville Prison, were displayed in various museums. To me those exhibits furthered the misshaped attitudes toward these veterans by determining that they were perhaps "freaks of nature". You may even remember that General Sickles himself added to the circus nature of these situations by actually contributing his missing limb to a museum.

As I prayed on this night, I asked the Father to soften peoples' hearts regarding these veterans who through no fault of their own returned home missing limbs. I felt that better attitudes of the people would greatly enhance the well-being of the veterans.

# Chapter 42
## Procedural Aspects of Amputation

April 1866

Our medical procedures have certainly progressed greatly since the Civil War. In fact, there were no Civil War procedures done with antiseptics, as Joseph Lister did not discover those until after the war was over. I have read too that of the 10,000 plus physicians in the North, only about 500 had ever performed surgery of any kind prior to their wartime assignments. By comparison, of the 3,000 Confederate doctors, only 27 had been documented as having performed surgery before the war. Since over 70% of all war wounds were to the extremities (arms and legs), a high percentage of Civil War doctors learned as they went along. And sometimes amputations were the most expedient answer to whatever the problem was.

Civil War surgeons would prepare for amputation by washing out the wound using a cloth which had often been used several times on other patients. He would probe the wound with either his finger or a probe from his medical kit, looking for bone, bullets or pieces of cloth in the wound. Both his finger and probe were likely to have been used before, like the cloth, without regard to cleaning them prior to going to the next patient. If the bone was broken or a trauma had occurred in a major blood vessel, the decision would be made to amputate.

Chloroform was the most common medicine used, unless, as in my case, the patient had lost too much blood to use anesthesia. The doctor would make two cuts, above and below the wound, and leave a flap of skin on one side. Using his bonesaw, he would saw through the bone quickly, often completing the operation in less than ten minutes. If you have heard the term "sawbones" it came from the doctor using that bonesaw. The doctor would often then toss the limb he removed onto a pile of similar objects from earlier in his long day.

In further explaining the procedure, the doctor cut completely through the bone and then would make an incision using his scalpel through the muscle and down to the bone. The surgeon would then tie off the arteries using horsehair, cotton, or silk thread. He would scrape the ends of the remaining bone smooth so that it would not poke back through the skin. The doctor would pull the flap of skin across the opening and sew it shut, leaving a stump and a hole for drainage.

Sometimes doctors covered the end of the stump with isinglass plaster or some other material to help it harden. In my case, they did not use anything of the sort. Again, I am not complaining, just informing. My doctor absolutely saved my life. And if Dr. Robison learned anything with my amputation that helped him with his next surgery, then good for him.

Make no mistake about it. The surgeon's goal was to save as many lives as possible. To accomplish that, many of the most injured patients, especially those with gut or head wounds, were bypassed and not treated at all. The surgeon was interested in helping as many men as he could in the least amount of time. He also could not afford spending time with those he determined had mortal wounds. That did not mean that particular soldier, deemed too far gone for medical treatment, actually died. Some did not.

The doctor's secondary concern after aiding the wounded was time management and getting the job done (including amputation) in the least amount of time.

Again, in my case, due to the small amount of wounded at Philippi in June 1861, Dr. Robison had time to spare. But when you consider surgeons at places like Gettysburg and Sharpsburg where the casualties exceeded 20,000, time was of the essence. Surgeons had no time for 45 minute amputations, the time it took Dr. Robison to cut off my leg. Most could complete five amputations in the same 45 minute time frame as the war went on.

Remember too that my amputation was Dr. Robison's first amputation. Most doctors later in the war were doing multiple amputations in a single day, had done hundreds at previous battles and needed to get them over with so that they could go on to the next patient.

Civil War surgeons were often criticized. I ran across this reference recently written in September 1862. Dr. Jonathon Letterman, medical director of the Army of the Potomac, addressed that issue in his battle report following the situation at Sharpsburg, Maryland where they had thousands of casualties. His letter stated the following:

*The surgery of these battlefields has been pronounced butchery. Gross misrepresentations of the conduct of medical officers have been made and scattered broadcast over the country, causing deep and heart-rending anxiety to those who had friends or relatives in the army, who might at any moment require the services of a surgeon. It is not to be supposed that there were no incompetent surgeons in the army. It is certainly true that there were; but these sweeping denunciations against a class of men who will favorably compare with the military surgeons of any country, because of the incompetency and short-comings of a few, are wrong, and do injustice to a body of men who have labored faithfully and well. It is easy to magnify an existing evil until it is beyond the bounds of truth. It is equally easy to pass by the good that has been done on the other side. Some medical officers lost their lives in their devotion to duty in the battle of Antietam, and others sickened from excessive labor which they conscientiously and skillfully performed. If any objection could be urged against the surgery of those fields, it would be the efforts on the part of surgeons to practice "conservative surgery" to too great an extent.*

I also read that Physician Oliver Wendell Holmes pointed out in 1863 that it was a common occurrence to have a friend or to know someone who had been disabled by the war, when a mere two years prior that would have been rare.

As always, I ended the day in prayer. Tonight I thanked God for the progress that had been made in the medical field. If something good had come out of the terrible Civil War, perhaps the improvement in medical procedures and understanding would be of utmost importance. Many more veterans with amputations would live due to those improved procedures.

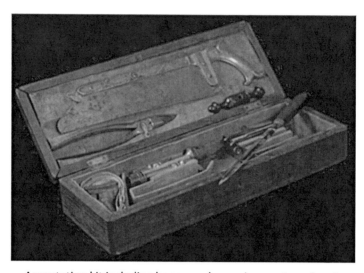

Amputation kit including bonesaw, bone nippers, tourniquet,
tweezers and other instruments
http://ncpedia.org/sites/default/files/images/ecu-
amputationkit.png

# Chapter 43
## More Aid Comes to Dismembered Soldiers

May 1867

My company's main competition for government contracts after the war ended was the company formed by Dr. Douglas Bly of Rochester, New York.

Dr. Bly was known for his invention, I'm thinking around 1858, of what he called "the most complete and successful invention ever attained in artificial limbs."

I continued to make improvements on the Hanger limb design. My improved leg design provided for replacing the catgut tendons with rubber bumpers. They were important to control dorsiflexion and plantar flexion. And I also designed a plug fit wood socket.

By March 1865, the federal government in Washington had set up the National Asylum for Disabled Volunteer Soldiers to take care of Union veterans. President Lincoln signed the legislation. He had said in his second Inaugural Address on March 4 that he saw a need for the country to care "for him who shall have borne the battle." Having met him and hearing of his support of government programs for dismembered veterans, his speech did not surprise me. Of note here was that Confederate veterans, like me, were not eligible for this type of government assistance.

In July of 1865 it was called to my attention that members of the Veterans Reserves (formerly the Invalid Corps) participated in the hangings of the Lincoln conspirators at Fort McNair in Washington, D.C. Their duty that day (July 7, 1865) was to knock the posts out from under the gallows to allow the conspirators (Mary Surratt, George Atzerodt, David Herod, and Lewis Powell) to fall to their deaths.

By 1866, North Carolina became the first state to offer artificial limbs for their veterans, providing free accommodations and transportation by rail to receive their prosthesis. Over 1,500 veterans received the offer from the state government through mail solicitation.

That same year, one fifth of the state of Mississippi's entire operating budget went to the purchase of prosthetic limbs for the state's wounded veterans.

U. S. Surgeon General J. K. Barnes established federal policy in May of 1866. That policy was reported in the following letter:

*SURGEON GENERAL'S OFFICE,*
*Washington, D. C.*

*May 11, 1866.*

*SIR: I have the honor to forward herewith the report called for by resolution of House of Representatives of April 10, 1866, received April 11, 1866. This report, commenced at once, was finished May 10, 1866, and embraces a list of manufacturers who are or have been authorized to furnish artificial limbs to soldiers at the expense of the government, with the names and residence of each soldier so supplied, the character of limb, and cost, covering 110 sheets of medium paper; it embraces 6,075 cases, viz: Arms, 2,134; legs,*

*3,784; hands, 44; feet, 9; apparatus, 104; total, 6,075, at a cost of $357,728.*

*Very respectfully, your obedient servant,*
*E. M. STANTON, Secretary of War.*
*J. K. BARNES, Surgeon General U. S. A.*

## ARTIFICIAL LIMBS FOR SOLDIERS

*The following is a list of all persons or firms, manufacturers of artificial limbs, who have been employed or authorized to furnish arms, legs, hands, or effect of their invention or construction to soldiers at the expense of the federal government: E. D. Hendsoll, New York City, New York; B. W. Jewett, Washington, D. C., B. Frank Palmer, Philadelphia, Pennsylvania; D. W. Kolbe, Philadelphia, Pennsylvania, Charles Stafford, Chicago, Illinois; Douglas Bly, New York City, New York; George B. Jewett, Salem, Massachusetts; M. A. Gildea, Philadelphia, Pennsylvania; Marvin Lincoln, Boston, Massachusetts; Small &, McMillen, Indianapolis, Indiana; William Selpho & Sons, New York City, New York; Salem Leg Company, Salem, Massachusetts; Jewett Leg Company, Washington, D. C.; Richard Clement, Philadelphia, Pennsylvania; A. A. Marks, New York City, New York; American Arm and Leg Company, Washington, D. C.; John Condell, Morristown, New York; National Arm and Leg Company, New York City, New York; J. Grenell & Company, New*

*York City, New York; E. Spellerberg, Philadelphia, Pennsylvania; B. W. Jewett Patent Leg Company, New York City, New York; and J. W. Weston, New York City, New York.*

I had remembered that Mr. Lincoln had suggested that my company would be able to sell to Union veterans too. With his unfortunate recent death, however, his endorsement would not matter.

Following that federal government edict, I corresponded with the Surgeon General's office to try to get my company listed as an acceptable provider for artificial limbs. Those companies listed had been receiving funding from the federal government to manufacture prosthetics for Union veterans and were obviously known prior to the end of the war as they were all located in the North.

In my letter, I pointed out the following:

1) my company had been manufacturing artificial limbs in Virginia since December of 1861
2) in 1863, I filed and received two patents with the Confederate government in Richmond for artificial legs
3) in March 1864, my company was one of just two companies who had been commissioned by the Association for the Relief of Maimed Soldiers (ARMS) to supply artificial legs to any dismembered Confederate veteran
4) my company had already provided artificial limbs through an exclusive contract with the Commonwealth of Virginia

5) the "Hanger" from which the Hanger limb was named came from my name
6) I had been the first amputee of the Civil War and for the record, my amputation occurred on June 3, 1861
7) I had been working on artificial limb designs daily since mid-1861
8) my company already had over 1,000 customers
9) I could furnish testimonials from most of my customers regarding their satisfaction with my company's work
10) I also attached references covering each point above

My company was quickly added as an officially recognized provider on the government's list following my letter, with a note of apology for their omission from the original list.

In his annual report in 1866, Secretary of War Edwin M. Stanton spelled out the government's policy by stating "the duty of the government to the soldiers who have been maimed or who have fallen in its defense has not been neglected. Much care has been taken, by precautions and practical tests, to secure for the former the most durable, useful and comfortable artificial limbs."

Initially Confederate veterans were not allowed to receive government benefits including artificial limbs. Some southern states stepped forward and established their own statewide programs.

The state of Georgia also established a program in 1866 to provide a free education to any indigent veterans under the age of 30 who had lost limbs.

In 1867, the general assembly of the state of Alabama voted to appropriate $30,000 for dismembered veterans.

Meanwhile, recently I had moved my limb factory to 1211½ E. Main Street in Richmond to be closer to the numerous hospitals in the capitol of the Commonwealth including the largest hospital in the South, Chimborazo Hospital, which had a capacity of 8,000 patients.

Ironically, several of my competitors had already set up shop on the same street including an agent for Dr. Bly who was located at 914 E. Main Street. I advertised my Hanger limbs as being superior to my competition due to my promise of a snug fit. Medical associations recommended Hanger legs as southern made and preferable to "the best Northern limbs."

I continued to boast that my Hanger limbs hid all signs of injury. My guarantee was always that Hanger limbs were comfortable, well-fitting and thoroughly tested. I made sure all potential customers knew that my patented socket had "no chafing, no jarring, no cords, no springs," and was always "the best and cheapest artificial leg."

And I continued to pray that the great God who had gotten me this far would keep me going as I seemed to be getting deeper involved in trying to help dismembered veterans live a productive life.

The Hanger Factory was located at 1211½ East Main Street in the Donnan-Asher Iron Front Building in Richmond's oldest mercantile center. The building still stands today.
http://www.nps.gov/nr/travel/richmond/StearnsDonnanAsher.html

# Chapter 44
## The Government Program Changes

By 1870, the federal government approved legislation to allow all veterans to have a choice. Veterans could now choose to receive either a replacement limb every three years or a government payment of $75. To qualify, veterans had to use an official application called the Application for Artificial Limb Commutation.

Although my company received plenty of business from that legislation, many veterans chose to take the money. It seemed that their financial troubles were even greater than their need for a replacement limb.

The government had already paid $500,000 by this time for 7,000 artificial limbs for Union soldiers.

As had been true all along, government officials continued to think that by giving veterans a new limb, the soldier's troubles would be over. That was far from the truth. Veterans also needed someone to make sure that their prosthesis fit, that they were comfortable, to help readjust it frequently, to help them find a job, and to support the additional problems that their injury brought into their lives.

Many men from both the South and the North refused to wear artificial limbs. Quite a few told me personally that they did not feel the need to receive what they considered charity from the government. Some chose to pin up their empty pant leg or empty shirt sleeve to make their honorable war sacrifice more visible.

Nurse Louisa May Alcott helped veterans missing limbs by saying often that "all women thought a wound the best decoration a brave soldier could wear." While I am not quite sure how Nurse Alcott knew the personal feelings of "all women", I certainly thought the concept was valid. And some told me they would have rather had their limb missing from a war injury than an industrial accident or having it taken off by an angry alligator.

I prayed that the government would continue to help those veterans in need, but would see the light that just a limb or some money was not the entire answer. To government officials I am thinking that they considered it was at least one answer. And like my original peg leg, I was appreciative that it was better than nothing. However, to James Hanger, the government programs were not that much better than nothing. I knew they needed to do better. I asked God to help me see to it that their programs did not stop short.

Lucius Fairchild, who had his left arm amputated following the action at Gettysburg in July 1863, chose to have an empty sleeve rather than a prosthetic arm.
www.nlm.nih.gov/exhibition/lifeandlimb/sacrificesforgotten.html

# Chapter 45
## Acceptance of My First U. S. Patent

I wrote to the U. S. Patent Office to try to secure copies of the two patents I had filed with the Confederate States of America Patent Office in 1863 for Hanger limbs. They were both for artificial legs. They were Patent No. 155 filed March 23, 1863 and Patent No. 201 filed August 18, 1863. It was my thought that by filing those applications with my upcoming application, it might hurry up the acceptance process.

Unfortunately, I was informed that most, if not all, of the Confederate patents had burned in a fire in Richmond during the evacuation of that city in March 1865.

In early 1871, I filed a patent with the U.S. Patent Office in Washington, D.C. It was approved February 14, 1871 and became designated as U.S. Patent No. 111,741 — J. E. Hanger Artificial Leg.

This leg weighed between eight and ten pounds. It was made from wood, leather, rubber, and steel springs. Its design included durability, stability, and motion and was a more lifelike Hanger limb than any I had designed to date.

As I look back to that first artificial Hanger leg I had built in my bedroom in Churchville, I had to laugh. My patented limb was at least a thousand times more practical and lifelike.

It was astounding to me how far I had come with God's grace and my God given ability to invent and construct. It had been just short of ten years since my accident at Philippi. I had come so far. I was truly blessed. My prayer this night was in gratitude for that grace and those talents.

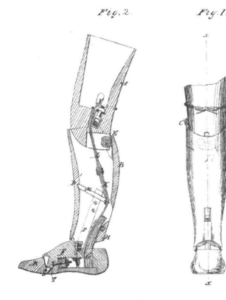

J. E. HANGER.
ARTIFICIAL LEG.

No. 111,741.

Patented Feb. 14, 1871.

U. S. Patent Office

# Chapter 46
## My Factory Opens in Churchville

In 1871, I returned to Churchville and started a factory in my home town. One of my first employees was Mike Sutton. I knew of his attitude and support of the prosthesis that he had now worn for just a shade less than ten years.

At this facility I would also produce limbs for veterans in need under my recent contract with the Commonwealth of Virginia. Staunton Mayor Nicholas K. Trout had been very instrumental in helping me secure that contract. Mayor Trout had written to state officials calling me both "a home manufacturer and maimed" and extolled the virtues of myself and my company as being superior to my main northern competitor, Mr. Bly. I will be forever indebted to Mayor Trout for his continued support for my factory in his town.

When I could, I made it a point to hire veterans with amputations. In my own personal experience, I found it quite useful when talking to a disabled veteran to show him my disability. I had determined that there could be no better salesman for my company's products than men who were already using a prosthesis that had improved their lives. Besides, many of these man had been out of work either by choice (thinking that they weren't capable of working a job) or where an employer wouldn't hire them due to their missing limb.

Mike Sutton, who was born missing a leg, could certainly relate better to veterans who had war related amputations than any man who had all his original, God provided extremities. Mike not only loved his job, but he was really good at it too.

I continued to tell anyone who would listen that having one leg did not define who these men were. And that these veterans were no less capable than they had been with two legs, except they might possibly move a bit slower. For some reason, folks often equated the lack of a limb with stupidity, surmising somehow that when these men had their amputation, their brains fell out too. It seemed to me that people perhaps thought a one-legged man might even be contagious and needed to be avoided.

While I found that quite hilarious in general, it was a sad statement for people who were quick to judge. Many "judged the book by the cover" so to speak, instead of letting these men get a fair shake.

I figured out early on that men with prosthetic limbs wanted to help others who needed artificial limbs. It was kind of a self-perpetuating stream of veterans helping veterans who in turn would want to help other veterans.

I prayed that my work would continue to make a difference as it had in these past ten years. God had not let my disability get in my way. He had, in fact, blessed me with abilities that I could make a difference in wounded veterans' lives. It was my calling. I was good at it. And I still wanted to carry on even further, with His support.

# Chapter 47
## New Veteran Problems Emerge

With the new plan to offer dismembered veterans the choice of receiving either a limb or the cash passed by Congress on June 8, 1872, men who had returned from the war and were dismembered had a new dilemma. They found themselves unable to provide for their families because they had no job. To them choosing the money was a better option. They could make do without the limb, as Mike Sutton had done throughout his life.

It was not surprising, then, that in general more veterans chose the money than the artificial limb. According to our company records, for both 1872 and 1873, my company provided 142 limbs for Virginians while an additional 432 chose the payments in lieu of taking a government provided limb.

By that same year, 1873, the U. S. Patent office had processed 133 patents for artificial limbs or some type of prosthesis since the war started in 1861.

I was not discouraged. In fact, their choices made perfect sense to me. Once again it all came back to having something that was better than nothing. Having cash to them was better than having nothing, even if they couldn't get around or work. Having a peg leg had been better than nothing for Mike Sutton, even when it had almost no functionality to it.

To me, a much better alternative would have been to provide a prosthesis plus the cash to all veterans rather than offering them one or the other. Of course, no one in the federal government had asked this rebel soldier my advice on this matter, or on any other related matter since President Lincoln had died.

As I think back on all that has come to fruition since 1861, progress is being made, slowly but surely. The government has set up programs and is providing the funding for some services. In my mind, they are certainly improving their offerings as the years go by. Those programs are not perfect, because they are still evolving. The procedures for amputations have improved. There have been many improvements in developing artificial limbs.

But we can do better on each and every one of those fronts. I pray that the government leaders push forward to continue to improve their programs. I pray that society is more acceptable in years to come for these heroic veterans who gave limbs to the cause they believed in and will have to live with their disability for the rest of their lives. And I pray that I will have the strength to keep on with my resolve to make a difference.

# Chapter 48
## Hanger Limbs Continued to Evolve

One veteran who had a Hanger limb, W. J. M. Young of Allegheny County, Virginia bragged that his leg was of smug fit and told anyone who would listen that as a Confederate veteran, he preferred to wear a southern-made leg. That was certainly supportive of my notion to not wear a Yankee peg leg.

As the years went by, I had determined how to take better care of my prosthetic limb and passed that knowledge on to my customers. For instance, I found that the elk skin bushing around the knee bolt needed to be lubricated (not oiled) about once a month. A small piece of tallow was one of the best lubricants, while graphite or Vaseline could answer to that purpose almost as well. About once every six months, men with prosthetic limbs needed to rub the leather parts including the leather straps on the suspenders with neat's foot oil or fish oil.

I also knew that most veterans with missing limbs needed a light limb, a comfortable limb, a durable limb and a quiet limb, all built into one device. The last specification came from my intimate knowledge of how noisy my Yankee peg leg had been. I was counting on the fact that veterans would want to buy their artificial limb from a reputable company they could count on as still being in business when they needed service following the fitting.

I was also certain that veterans would want some kind of guarantee that if their leg limb broke or needed any kind of adjustment, they wouldn't have to go far or pay anything for the service. The Hanger Company was one of the few companies from the beginning who offered all of the above.

I had determined long ago that my best customer was a satisfied customer. He would be someone who would tell anyone inquiring that he was wearing a Hanger limb and that he was pleased with the limb. Anything else was not acceptable to me. By contrast, someone not satisfied would be just as quick to tell everyone inquiring that he was wearing a Hanger limb and that he was not satisfied. That bad publicity would be a deadly blow to my company. We could not withstand much of that. There was too much competition in the country.

I wanted to establish the best, most highly regarded, and most service oriented artificial leg company around. I would not settle for second best or just good enough. If I had any fault, it was in telling my employees perhaps too many times that Hanger limbs had the best guarantee in the country and each and every one of them personally had a stake in standing behind that guarantee.

I prayed unceasingly that I would be able to overcome any personal doubt and that by the grace of God I could carry on the high standards that I strongly believed in.

# Chapter 49
## My Marriage to Nora McCarthy

In the early 1870s, I had started courting Nora Slater McCarthy. She was the daughter of Edward H. and Princetta H. McCarthy of Richmond. Her father was a U. S. Customs officer.

Nora was 20 years old and eleven years younger than me. She was much more refined and educated too. She was a graduate of Hollins Institute, a fine women's college in Roanoke, Virginia where she received a departmental diploma in French Language and Literature in June of 1868.

It had been a real stretch for many years for me to court anyone for several reasons. I was fiercely independent and set in my ways. I did not need anyone's help at any time and for any reason. I tended to think of myself as a loner and was not sure anyone would be able to partner with me on any level. I was not even sure a woman of stature would be willing to accept my misfortune of the war.

Taking all that in mind, I talked myself into the situation by thinking in exactly the opposite direction. I counted my assets. I doubted anyone who saw me get around or maintain my productive life would have said that James Hanger had any kind of physical disability. I was both a successful business man and a good citizen. I was fairly good looking and definitely good natured. I was kind spirited and always willing to help someone in need. Not too many things bothered me. I was a good problem solver. I was smart. I was trustworthy.

When I looked at all my positive assets, I determined that I would indeed be a good catch. Fortunately for me, Nora McCarthy had figured that out on her own, without any help from me at all. She didn't ask me to submit a list of my assets. Apparently they were fairly obvious to her.

There was one thing for sure I could say about Nora. She never, not even once, gave any notice to my lack of having two good legs. In fact, she made mention later that she had absolutely not noticed my artificial leg at all when we first met.

We were married on October 21, 1873 in Richmond, Virginia by Reverend J. Peterkin.

Nora was a good cook, a good listener, and an outstanding companion. Where she was a good thinker, I was a good doer. And actually that made for a very workable combination in our lives.

Along the way, she learned to love me for who I was, not for what limb I had or did not have. And from the first, she was extremely supportive of my work both with Hanger limbs and with caring for the veterans who needed them.

She often said, "James. I truly believe you would be helping these veterans regardless of whether you owned the company or developed the patent or not. It is in your blood to make sure these men are provided for."

She was right in that regard. I thought mostly that I was providing a valuable and necessary service. I did not consider it a job, and, in fact, my attitude in that regard was more than likely a hindrance than an advantage to good business practices.

That same year, Congress changed the name of the National Asylum to the National Home for Disabled Volunteer Veterans and provided prosthetic limbs for all veterans. That included those often left out veterans who had served in the Confederacy. In my mind, the policy change had been a long time coming. As Dr. Robison would have said, the color of the uniform had absolutely no bearing on the needs of those returning from the war. They were all Americans. To me, they all deserved to be helped.

I prayed nightly with Nora following our marriage. We were spiritually connected for sure. At this time in my life I prayed in gratitude that Nora, another of God's angels, had been sent to me just about the time when I needed her the most. I was thankful that the Lord knew my needs in that regard long before I realized them. And I asked His help in being a good husband to Nora.

# Chapter 50
## New Federal Programs are Developed

In 1876, a veteran, John S. Robson of the 52$^{nd}$ Virginia Infantry, whose leg had been amputated due to a war wound, wrote a book called "How a One-legged Rebel Lives". In the book Corporal Robson offered that he found "this world a pretty hard place to flourish when you have no money and one leg to make it with." He saw selling his book as his last possible chance to become self-sufficient.

Robson, who wore a Hanger limb, wrote "Could I find employment in any way, I assure my readers I would not resort to authorship, but in these days of depression, when so many young and willing persons, sound of mind and whole in limb, are out of employment and can find nothing to do, my chances are hopeless indeed. For hard and laborious work, I am physically unfit and few would be willing to pay me reasonable wages."

By 1880, veterans were receiving pensions that included extra benefits if they were missing a limb or several limbs. But unlike Dr. Robison, the federal government was not as generous with pensions to the boys in gray who lost the war. Pensions for those Union soldiers who lost an arm, for instance, were around $432 per year. For the same type of dismemberment, Confederate veterans received $50 annually.

That was not a surprise to me at all. It probably didn't surprise any of the Confederate veterans either.

Let there be no mistake about it. Even now, fifteen long years following the war, there were still officials in key positions in the federal government who had personal agendas calling for retribution and punishment against the South.

I wondered when, if ever, those famous words in the Declaration of Independence "all men are created equal" actually would be put into practice.

In 1880, the state of Louisiana enacted legislation that provided for artificial limbs or a cash payment for their veterans of the war. Their appropriation for covering that program was $12,000 for the first year and $8,000 for 1881. During 1882 they appropriated $1,300 for artificial limbs, $1,000 for limb repair and followed that the next year by providing $1,300 for artificial limbs and $1,071 for repairs to those limbs. For 1884 and 1885, that appropriation had risen to $8,000 each year. The state had contracted with A. McDermott of New Orleans to provide those prosthetic limbs.

I prayed in thanksgiving that programs continued to be developed, but at the same time asked God to hurry officials up in making them fair to all veterans, not just the favored victors in blue. As you know by now, I am not always patient in these regards. And I asked God for more patience.

# Chapter 51
## My Return Visit to Philippi

June 1, 1881

I decided earlier this year that I wanted to go back to visit Philippi, Virginia. I wanted to revisit the barn where I got injured and where my amputation took place. I had thought about it every day for twenty years. I had in mind visiting the church where I had recuperated and to visit with the McClaskey and Hite families to thank them again. I certainly wanted to return to see Samuel. When I had left, he asked that I return someday. And above all, I wanted to share all those important places with Nora.

I had written notes to William McClaskey and Thomas Hite. Both wrote back saying they were happy to hear that we planned to visit. They provided directions so I could find their homes. Thomas Hite said Samuel, now 26 years old, was particularly excited that I was returning.

I prayed that I could handle whatever happened on that upcoming trip.

June 17, 1881

Nora and I left Churchville in our buggy to go to Philippi. The drive took four days. On the way I wondered how I would be feeling when I got there. That short time in my life certainly didn't turn out anything like I would have ever imagined. Nora asked me if it would be difficult for me to cover that ground again. I told her truthfully that I was not sure at all what this trip was going to bring to me. I just knew I had to revisit.

June 21, 1881

We arrived in Philippi in the early morning. I asked directions and then drove the buggy directly to the Garrett Johnson farm. I knocked on the door and asked for Mr. Johnson. An elderly gentleman came to the door. He said he was Mr. Johnson. I introduced myself and my wife, telling him who I was and why I was here. He invited us to come in and sit down.

"You are a legend in this town, Mr. Hanger," Mr. Johnson said. "The first amputee of the War Between the States. I had heard the accident and the amputation of your injured leg had taken place in my barn. You look like you are doing well." He was looking me over, likely trying to see if he could figure out which of my legs had been lost in his barn. I don't think he could figure it out.

"The action that took place here in your barn and in Philippi changed my life forever," I explained. "I now am a businessman. I didn't volunteer for the distinction or the fame. But I have made the best of it. My company provides artificial limbs for veterans from both the North and the South."

I rolled up my pant leg and showed him my Hanger limb. I continued. "I think some good has come out of that crazy war. I would like to show Nora the barn." I rolled my pants back down.

"Do you mind if I walk with you?"

"Of course not."

He walked to the door of his house and held it for us. He led us to the barn. The closer I got to the building, the harder my heart began to race.

When we walked into the barn, it looked just like I had remembered all these years. There was nothing unique about it. I certainly remembered being in this barn before. I didn't have to say anything to Nora. She knew the story. The barn was where the wayward cannon ball had mangled my leg. This was where the men had lifted me onto what I was told was a door. And this is where Dr. Robison's surgery had saved my life.

I had to lean on the wall to hold myself up. I started to quietly cry. I was embarrassed, but could not stop. I tried to remember the excruciating pain I must have felt or the horrible sound of the doctor's bone saw cutting through my leg. I could not remember either.

But I did remember Dr. Robison's description of the operation and the pain that I endured for weeks and weeks afterwards. It seemed so real, like it was happening all over again. I crumpled onto the floor. Nora stood by quietly. I cried loudly, unable to stop. My thoughts of what happened here enveloped me. I was unable to move.

Dr. Robison's face appeared clearly in my mind. He had been so calm in telling me several days later what had happened. He acted like it was routine – no big thing. Yet he must have been afraid too. That was his first amputation. I had not felt even one thread of doubt that he had done the best he could. His determination and confidence helped calm my fears. Dr. Robison was a Union doctor who had operated on a Confederate soldier. I still have problems imagining that just any Union doctor would have tried to save me. After all, I was the enemy. Yet Dr. Robison had conducted the operation, as he said, the same as if I had been his own son. And his successful surgery had pretty much been an integral part of every other step that I had taken in the last twenty years. I owed him everything.

I was so overcome with emotion that I was unsure if I could go on. I had to take deep breaths to bring myself back into the present.

Nora stood beside me as she had for so many years. She had heard my story. We both had wondered what would happen when I returned. Now we knew. It had been exhausting for me.

I finally struggled to get up. Nora knew I had to do this on my own, but held out her hand. She wanted me to know it was there, even if I wasn't going to take it. This time I did take it. I let her help me up. She held me tight for several minutes to let me know that everything was all right.

We finally moved on. I was still shaken, but knew I had to leave.

My wife wondered out loud if going into the barn had jarred my memory. She asked me if I remembered getting hit by the cannonball or going through the operation.

"Not really," I admitted. "And perhaps it is a good thing that I don't remember."

We walked back to the buggy. I thanked Mr. Johnson. And we left. I turned the buggy and travelled across the long covered bridge. I asked a lady on the street to point out the United Methodist Episcopal Church on Church Street in the downtown.

I drove the buggy to the front of the church. I helped Nora down and walked to the front to look around. I tried the door. It was locked. I told Nora to wait. I walked slowly to the house nearby hoping that someone could let us into the church. I knocked on the door.

I identified myself to the elderly lady who answered the door. I asked for Reverend Hindman who had been pastor in 1861. She said he was long gone, that her husband was pastor now, but was not at home.

I told her of my mission today, to visit the church where I had been when it was a Civil War hospital. She said she would gladly let me into the building. She excused herself and came back with a large key.

I walked with her back to the church. I introduced her to Nora. She opened the door and let us in and then excused herself. "Stay as long as you want," she told us. "I have chores to do. I will come back later and lock up. God Bless."

At first my legs didn't want to take me into the building. It was a strange feeling. I almost had to push myself in through the door.

The church looked the same as I had remembered. I walked in and sat down on the bench where I had laid during my stay here. Tears came to my eyes. Nora came close and put her hand on my shoulder. She didn't need to say anything. There was nothing she could have said.

I closed my eyes. I was back there in the church, twenty years ago, in pain, wondering if I was going to even live for another day. I was just trying to survive. Sweat was rolling down my face now. The discomfort was almost unbearable. I wanted to run away while at the same time knowing that I needed to stay. I "saw" Deborah's face, the angel who had comforted me so many years ago. I envisioned Reverend Hindman praying with me and for me.

I stayed for a long time. I was not sure how long. Nora showed no impatience at all. I was grateful. The memories flooded back. I could smell the old hospital. I could hear the sounds of the wounded men around me. I could even feel an itching in my missing foot, a feeling that I had not felt in years. The bench was as hard as I remembered. The same bench that Rev. Hindman said was purposely uncomfortable so parishioners wouldn't fall asleep during church services. Yet I had slept on this bench.

I finally was able to stand up and walk out of the church. The McClaskey family was waiting for us. I helped Nora into the buggy and climbed on board. Then I drove to the McClaskey's home.

Nora asked if I were all right. I thanked her for asking and noted that I was exhausted, but otherwise was glad to be here today.

We arrived at their home around noon. Before my buggy stopped, I noticed a handsome couple waiting patiently on the porch. I pulled the buggy to a stop and got out, helping Nora get down too. Sheriff William and his wife Catherine greeted me. I introduced them to Nora.

Catherine apologized that none of the girls were able to be here, though she said several of their seven girls and their families were scheduled to stop by later. And she also said she had been embarrassed that her girls were afraid of me because of my missing limb during my stay with their family.

I explained that phenomenon was not uncommon at all and pretty much came with the territory for me.

We chatted outside on the porch. William asked what had happened to me after I left Philippi. I gave him the condensed version including my short time in prison. My tale ended with me reaching down and rolling up my pant leg to proudly show off my Hanger limb. They seemed quite amazed.

Mr. McClasky said he had been embarrassed that my stay with them had been cut short. He told us that the federals, after chasing the local units of rebels out of Philippi, had commandeered their house and used it for their headquarters for several months. "If we hadn't hated the Yankees up to that point, their upending my family and moving them out and then desecrating our house and property provided more than enough reasons. They even held me prisoner for a while as if I were a common criminal."

Catherine said that she had prepared a huge feast. She invited us inside. We talked and laughed and caught up. Her food was as good as I had remembered and that I had told Nora about. After lunch she gave us a tour of the house, stopping to show Nora where the bedroom was where they had cared for me. Later Mattie and her husband and children Harry, Nettie and Frank, and her younger sister, Rebecca, stopped by too. Mattie's family lived in nearby Grafton. Rebecca was a music teacher who lived with her sister's family. It was nice to see them again. They too seemed real happy that I was doing so well.

At about 4 o'clock, we thanked the McClaskey family and wished each other well. I helped Nora into the buggy. I turned north and headed for the Hite family home at Cherry Hill.

Once again we were greeted enthusiastically before the buggy stopped. A handsome young man about 26 years old stood out a dozen or so feet in front of his father, Thomas and his mother, Evaline. I knew it was Samuel.

When the buggy stopped and I hit the ground, Samuel was right there, holding his hand out for me to shake. I had taken the crooked metal cross he had presented to me so many years ago out of my pocket and put it in my right hand. When we shook, he felt the cross first. And he smiled.

"I hated that table leg that you wore when you were here, sir," Samuel said, speaking excitedly. "You look like you have two good legs now. I am grateful that you have returned. I have thought of you often for twenty years. It is great seeing you."

"Samuel. You have grown to become a man. I have prayed with this cross every single night for twenty years. I have practically worn it out. So you see. I definitely have not forgotten about you either."

Evaline gave us the quick house tour, pointing out to Nora the bedroom where I had stayed. It had been a comfortable place for me to stay, being much more comfortable than my hard bench at the church or my bunk bed at Camp Chase after I left.

In our conversation, Thomas said the war hadn't stayed long in Philippi. They were grateful. His father had passed away. His other children were grown with families of their own. Only Samuel was able to come to see us today. His father added that Samuel would not have missed this day for anything.

"We are blessed that you have returned, Mr. Hanger," he said. "And we are pleased that you have turned the accident at Philippi into something useful. Several local men could certainly use your services."

I asked Samuel if he remembered looking for my lost leg. He seemed embarrassed while shaking his head yes. "That was totally my fault," I told him. "I didn't realize when I told you that I had lost my leg that you would take it literally. Do you want to see my new leg?"

Samuel said no. I don't think he wanted to embarrass me. It wasn't embarrassing to me at all. I was proud to show anyone and everyone my invention. I wanted to show him and his family as much as anyone because I was darn proud of my accomplishments. I stood up and rolled up my pant leg.

"You know if I had not been hit in Philippi, veterans across the country would not have Hanger limbs," I explained. "What could have been a tragedy, pretty much ruining my life, instead became a tremendous opportunity for me. I am truly blessed." I explained how my leg worked, showing them the hinged knee and the lateral movement at the ankle.

Samuel seemed impressed. "It is certainly a great improvement over that table leg that you wore. If I ever lost my leg, I would be proud to wear a Hanger limb."

We talked for hours. It was so late that we ended up staying the night. Nora and I slept in the same bed I slept in when I stayed with the Hite family in 1861.

June 22, 1881

Following a good night's sleep and a fine breakfast, we said goodbye. It was time to go back home to Churchville. When I helped Nora board the buggy, Samuel stayed close by. He hugged me tightly. "Thank you, Mr. Hanger, for visiting me. All my life I have waited for this day. We will meet again."

I held up that crooked little cross. "I cherish my memories of you, Samuel. I am blessed by your gift every day. It connects me back to those times when I didn't think I would even live another day. It has given me the faith to go on. Thank you for that."

As Nora and I returned toward home, she asked me if the trip had been as meaningful as I might have anticipated.

It was so much more. I needed to reconnect with those days in Philippi, with the places and with the people. "Thank you for going along, Nora." I said. "Your presence there alongside me made it even more special."

My prayer was in extreme gratitude to God for all that had happened for the last twenty years in my life. I gave thanks for how the story had turned out following what certainly could have been James Hanger's death at Philippi.

# Chapter 52
## The International
## Cotton Exposition of 1881

After returning to Churchville from Philippi, I travelled to the city of Atlanta, Georgia where they were hosting the International Cotton Exposition. The fair, which was open from October 5 to December 3, was held at Oglethorpe Park. Although the exhibits were initially to show the progress made by the city of Atlanta since its destruction during the Civil War and developments in cotton production, the concept was broadened to include exhibits concerning railroads, horticulture, arts, and industry. My company's exhibit showing the progress made in the development of artificial limbs was a prize winner.

A man stopped at the Hanger Company booth at the exposition and asked to speak to me by name. I had just finished my conversation with a potential customer who was a veteran from the Georgia Infantry who had been wounded at Sharpsburg, Maryland in September, 1862 and was missing his right leg. I approached the man who was inquiring.

A distinguished looking gentleman with white hair and a full beard held his hand out to greet me. He was smiling from ear to ear. He asked if I remembered him. He certainly looked familiar.

"Philippi, Virginia," he said. "June 3, 1861."

I was taken back. "Dr. James Robison. Oh my God. The man who saved my life." I grabbed his hand and pulled him close. "It is great to see you. My wife, Nora, and I had been recently discussing you and your work. We just visited Philippi again in June and stopped by the barn where the amputation had taken place."

"I remember you as a pretty determined soldier, Mr. Hanger," Dr. Robison offered. "I see that you have done well for yourself. I remember that you told me that you were going to live a long time. I have read in the newspapers that your artificial legs are sought by veterans all over the country."

"You don't know the half of it," I said with a chuckle. "Let me show you something." I took off my pants, in front of Dr. Robison and all of the world. I did not care. I sat down and took off my prosthesis. And then I motioned for him to come close so I could show him my stump.

"Doctor. Look at your work. For someone who had never done an amputation before, thank God you had at least read up on the matter. You performed admirably. Besides saving my life, you provided me with a stump that healed and gave me a place to attach an artificial leg."

He closely examined what remained of my left leg, a heeled and hardened stump. And then I reattached my artificial leg and let him examine it too. I pointed out the hinged knee and the rotating ankle. He seemed impressed.

Dr. Robison explained that he was at a medical conference this week in Atlanta. Officials at his conference had encouraged their participants to come to look at the medical advances shown in some of the booths at the exposition. When he saw the name Hanger Company and that we offered prosthetic limbs, he had some inkling that he might know something about Mr. Hanger himself.

The doctor told me he had returned to his hometown of Wooster, Ohio when his 90 day enlistment was over to become a physician and surgeon. He admitted that he had done other amputations during the war, but for some reason his thoughts always returned to his first one. He said he had wondered over the years what had happened to that determined Virginia cavalry soldier named James Hanger. Now he knew, and he expressed how proud he was to have had some small part in the success of my company.

I expanded on that thought. "You have not been a small part of my company's success, but rather you have made a difference not only in my life but in the lives of thousands of dismembered Civil War veterans on both sides of the conflict. To me, your part was certainly not small at all, but huge. If it weren't for you, Dr. Robison, there would be no Hanger limbs because there would be no James Hanger. It is as simple as that."

He seemed embarrassed by the praise. I continued, "I have always been curious about something. What were you thinking when you started on your first amputation? Were you frightened or nervous?"

He laughed. "Truthfully, I was probably more scared than you were, Mr. Hanger," he admitted. "I took being a surgeon very seriously then and I still do now. I always wanted my patients to survive their operations. I was not sure that you had much chance. But I knew if I didn't take your leg off, you had no chance at all. You would not have survived the night. After a few seconds into the procedure, my fears went away. I was too busy trying to figure out how to take care of my young patient than to worry about my personal doubt."

"I remember you telling me that I fussed something terrible during the operation," I continued.

"That you did," he said with a chuckle. "You had many choice words for me that I would not repeat. I was too focused on the surgery to pay close attention. Luckily I had several strong boys from my regiment who held you down and kept you fairly still. You were in intense pain. You had lost too much blood. I was afraid to give you chloroform."

"I understand the oath you took as a doctor, but I am still amazed that a Union doctor took such good care of his enemy," I told him. "Now I am in the same boat. Because of your influence, I have absolutely no problem providing artificial limbs to soldiers who wore either colored uniform."

By that time the doctor said he had a meeting to attend. We shook hands heartily and wished each other well. It had been such a blessing to see him again.

My only regret was that I was just sorry Nora was not here today to meet the man who saved my life so many years ago. I was grateful to God that Dr. Robison had shown up again in my life so that I could thank him for prolonging my life.

Dr. James D. Robison
http://www.mkwe.com/ohio/pages/H005-00.htm

# Chapter 53
## The Hanger Company Expands

By 1883, I had established another office, in Washington, D.C. at 207 4 1/2 Street N.W. and called it James E. Hanger Inc. It was just four doors north of Pennsylvania Avenue, a fine location in the nation's capital. Our home was by this time located at 2726 N. Street NW.

As the years went by, more and more of the southern states passed legislation supporting their dismembered veterans. In 1886, the state of Louisiana, under Act #115, gave land grants of 160 acres to wounded and disabled veterans or to their widows.

In 1887, the state of Georgia declared an annual pension for a man who had lost one arm or one leg to be $150.

In 1890, our company expanded significantly. I moved my corporate headquarters to 417 11th Street, NW, Washington, D. C.

As per always, I prayed in thanksgiving that God continued to bless us with more and more business. And that I was up to being able to handle the work load that the expanded business opportunity provided.

# Chapter 54
## More Help for Confederate Veterans

The Association of the Confederate Veterans was established in 1890 for two main purposes – to collect and preserve the records of the medical corps of the Confederate army and navy and to determine the number and condition of surviving Confederate veterans who had been disabled by wounds and disease during the conflict.

The report of that organization indicated that the Medical Corps of the Confederate army treated more than three million cases of wounds and disease between 1861 and 1865. They estimated that out of about 600,000 men actually engaged in battles, a total of 194,026 suffered wounds and were treated by 834 surgeons and 1,668 assistant surgeons, with one surgeon and two assistant surgeons assigned to each command.

The records from the Commonwealth of Virginia for their soldiers who fought and became disabled as a result of fighting for the Old Dominion had all been lost. In correspondence regarding the information sought from each Confederate state by the Association of the Confederate Veterans from James McDonald, Adjutant-General, McDonald explained

> *"Your letter of the 17th instant to Governor McKinney, requesting information as to the number of troops from Virginia in the Confederate armies; character of their organizations; numbers killed, wounded, died of*

*disease, deserted; roster of medical officers, etc., etc., has been referred to me for reply.*

*I regret extremely to have to say that it is not possible to give this information. In the great fire that attended the evacuation of this city by the Confederate forces, April 3, 1865, the office of the adjutant-general, with its entire contents, was destroyed. Whatever records or files it contained capable of throwing light on the subject of your inquiries, were thus lost forever. Of course, also, all headquarters' records and papers with our armies in the field were turned over to United States officers, to whom they surrendered, and are now in Washington.*

*There is in this state one Soldiers' Home for disabled Confederates. It is located in the suburbs of Richmond and affords accommodations to about one hundred and thirty inmates. The state appropriates ten thousand dollars a year to their maintenance. Besides, some seventy thousand dollars a year are appropriated for the relief of Confederate veterans disabled by wounds received in service. There are a number of Confederate camps in various parts of the state, the principal one being R. E. Lee Camp, in this city, by which maintenance is given to needy veterans.*"

Of interest in the above letter, paragraph two, is the use of the word "inmates" to describe Civil War veterans convalescing in the Soldier's Home. This goes back to what I had discussed before. There is a feeling by some in society that persons missing a limb are "contagious" or a danger to themselves and that their disability made them risks to society on some level.

While I was extremely grateful to God for his blessings on officials to see the need for veteran programs, the war had ended in 1865. It had been 25 years. Why was more not being done? I asked the Heavenly Father to give me patience to endure the slow pace of government officials, while at the same time asking Him to push for more, not for me, but for those men still in extreme hardship for too many years already.

# Chapter 55
## Filing Another Artificial Leg Patent

I filed another patent for an artificial leg in Washington, D. C. at the Patent Office on November 7, 1891. It was accepted on December 22, 1891. The patent, and its official U. S. Patent No. 465,698, specified that "my invention relates to improvements in artificial legs, the object being to provide an improved construction of the knee and ankle joints and of the socket, whereby superior advantages are attained with respect to simplicity, efficiency and comfort of the wearer."

Each of my patents was designed to offer improvements on my previous patents, or a patent filed by someone else.

I wish I would have kept all the drawings I had made in 1861 of my first leg and every change I had made since. In the ensuring thirty years, I probably have drawn over a thousand different models. Each one was a tad better than the one before it. You cannot imagine how much progress I have made over those years.

God had provided me with both the expertise to continue to develop better and better Hanger limbs and had allowed me to survive the war to carry on my work. I was blessed with both. But I was still not finished.

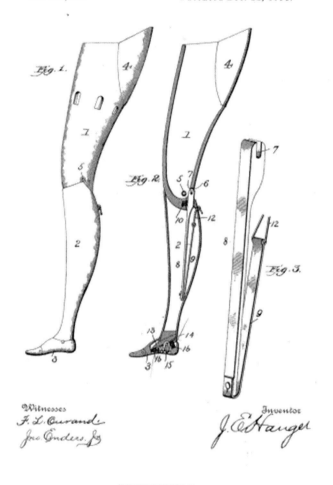

(No Model.)

J. E. HANGER.
ARTIFICIAL LEG.

No. 465,698.

Patented Dec. 22, 1891.

Witnesses

Inventor
J. E. Hanger

U.S. Patent Office

192

# Chapter 56
## Sad News Arrives from Ohio

May 24, 1895

I was informed by letter from his family today that Dr. James D. Robison passed away on May 9, 1895. He was 75 years old.

I had to sit down to process the sad news. Dr. Robison was the single most important person in my life. He was in June of 1861. He still was. With every single solitary second step I have taken since that day and his successful operation, I have silently thanked God for sending this fine doctor to rescue and save me.

I cried softly, not for the loss but for all the blessings that his work had brought to my life. I cannot imagine who I would have become or what I would have been doing today if it hadn't been for Dr. Robison. Ironically, in taking my leg he had given me everything.

Nora came into the sitting room, and like always, put her hand on my shoulder. She didn't say a word. But it was comforting that she was there with me. I handed her the letter. All she said was, "Oh, how dreadful."

And it was indeed dreadful news. She asked me if I wanted to talk about it. I shook my head back and forth. I wasn't ready for that.

I sat quietly and let myself revisit the barn where the amputation had taken place. I remembered the moment Dr. Robison explained to me that he had read up on amputations but that mine had been his first one. He promised that he had treated me as if I were his own son.

He also said that if anyone could have done my surgery correctly, it would have been him.

For some reason, this rebel soldier trusted that the Union surgeon had done as well as he could. In truth, I had had no other choice. He said I would more than likely have died without the amputation, and I surely hadn't wanted to die.

I am so grateful that I had gotten to reconnect with Dr. Robison in Atlanta several years back. I wish I would have kept track over all these years of all the soldiers Dr. Robison has indirectly aided by saving my life. I know it has been thousands.

Dr. Robison can surely rest in peace knowing that his one action made a world of difference in many people's lives. And I will continue to be eternally grateful for the fact that he had truly saved my life. I thanked God for Dr. Robison, for his successful surgery, and for being able to reconnect with him in Atlanta.

# Chapter 57
## Speaking Opportunities in Ohio

In the summer of 1901 I received a letter from a member of the 16th Ohio Volunteer Infantry inviting me to come to Ohio to speak at their veterans' reunion the week of September 9, 1901 in Cleveland, Ohio. I was happy to go. The 16th Ohio Infantry had long been my favorite Union regiment. In fact, most Confederate soldiers do not have a favorite Union regiment. They were my favorites because they were the boys who found me injured in the barn that fateful day in Philippi in 1861. They summoned Dr. Robison, their regimental surgeon. And he had saved my life. Even with Dr. Robison's recent death, I was excited to speak to them and thank them.

Nora supported my trip there and went along. At the event, several veterans said they had been at the scene and had been the ones who found me and went for help. Nora and I were treated very specially by the boys from Ohio forty years after the actual event, even though I had been a soldier on the Confederate side and could have still been considered their enemy.

The 16th Ohio Volunteer Infantry was evidently more impressed with my talk than they had expressed at the time. They invited me to return the following year to speak at the Grand Army of the Republic state convention in Akron, Ohio on August 6, 1902. And once again I graciously accepted the invitation.

At both meetings I said pretty much the same thing. I thanked the boys of the 16th Ohio Volunteer Infantry first for finding me in the barn and secondly for summoning Dr. Robison. I told them that I did not remember what happened, but shared with them a letter I had received following the incident from Billy Davis of the 7th Indiana Infantry who had also been present that day.

Here's what Billy said he saw. "In this stable is where a rebel soldier lost a leg by a solid shot from our artillery. Here we found him. See here this blood. He ran here to get his horse. Dr. New assisted to amputate his limb."

In each case I added a shortened version of Dr. Robison's description of my amputation, my convalescence, and my invention of the Hanger limb. And then I rolled up my pant leg and showed them my invention as I reminded them that none of this ever could have happened without their finding me and starting the process back in 1861.

I told of my amazement that a Union doctor would amputate an enemy soldier's leg and of my joy of getting to talk to Dr. Robison not too long before his death. And I spoke of the repercussions, still reverberating today by the events of the day in which some of them, their friends, and neighbors certainly participated fully. I was certain they had no idea that the humane act of finding me and summoning help had enabled thousands of Union and Confederate veterans to be walking on artificial limbs today.

At the end of my talk, I dramatically reached into my bag and pulled out the actual wayward cannon ball a Churchville Cavalry soldier had retrieved from the barn that morning and presented to me following the war. I showed it off proudly. It was a solid 6 pounder, about 3 ½ inches in diameter.

Nora complained both times that showing them the cannon ball was over dramatic. I had thought it was a fine ending to my presentations.

Upon returning home, I again called on the Lord. I thanked him for the unique opportunity for presenting to those outstanding members of the 16th Ohio Volunteer Infantry who could have killed me in that barn but didn't. They could have ignored my wounding but called on their surgeon instead. I am living proof of their actions, and I will remain forever grateful. And I asked God to continue to bless the boys of the 16th Ohio Volunteer Infantry.

6 Pounder -- Civil War Cannon Ball
www.icollector.com

# Chapter 58
## Other Interests of Mine

You may be surprised to know that artificial limbs were not my only interest. I also invented a shampoo bowl attachment for a barber's chair, several adjustable reclining chairs, a rotary engine, a baling press, a fly-fan attachment for a table that chased those pesky flies away, and a lathe needed to manufacture the artificial limbs. And I have the U. S. patents to prove them all. I founded a company in West Virginia in 1896 called the Hanger Shampoo Bowl Company.

I always was more interested in helping people in need than making money manufacturing prosthetic limbs, just as my wife, Nora, had said on many occasions.

I recently encountered a legless colored man in Washington, D.C. who was begging for alms near the capitol. I sat on the ground next to him. I showed him my prosthetic leg. I told him my story. I told him I would make two artificial legs for him at no cost if he promised me that he would wear them.

He was skeptical, for sure. He did not trust me, or anyone for that matter. I couldn't imagine why he would trust a stranger. But after I sat and talked to him for a dozen or so times, he started appreciating my visits. And he agreed to be measured for two prosthetic legs. I worked with him on measurements and then came back with my sons. My sons carried him to our office where we fitted him with two new legs.

I encouraged him to walk on them often. When I stopped by the next week to his location on the sidewalk, he was still begging. His new Hanger limbs were nowhere in sight. He was not willing to talk to me. But that didn't discourage me as it might someone else. I stopped back again and again. Finally he came clean.

"Massa Hanger," he said. "This is all I know how to do. Been doin' it all the days of my entire life. If I wear my new legs here, no one's gonna feel sorry for me anymore. My hat will be empty. I's gonna be outta business. Massa Hanger. Do not think I am not grateful. I is. When I's walkin in my house, I feel like a new man. I is totally grateful. You understand me?"

He was right. Having legs was going to put him out of the begging business. And while he thought that was a bad thing, I was thinking the opposite. I offered him a job with our company. Again he was skeptical.

"What's I gonna do for you, Massa Hanger?"

"I am sure you can work for me as a janitor. I pay well. But this isn't going to be charity."

Like most others, he was not interested in the cosmetic features of his new limbs. Most men missing a limb over the years had the same things in mind – they wanted some way to improve their mobility and be able to return to the workforce in order to regain a sense of self sufficiency.

He needed some time to consider. He was friendly each time I stopped at his corner. We never discussed the fact that he wasn't wearing his new limbs, that he was still begging, or that there was a job offer in the waiting.

I stopped to visit almost every single day. I was careful not to push him. I knew he would decide when he was good and ready. I was a salesman first, as I always had been. And as I had always taught my sons, enthusiasm was about half of all salesmanship.

Eventually he did accept a position with the company. I took great solace in watching him climb stairs and in time, climb a ladder with relative ease. He became a trusted janitor with my company and a valuable employee. All he needed was a chance. And every time he saw me, he thanked me.

Since that day in Philippi, Virginia, when a wayward cannon ball found me, I have continued to be thankful for the great opportunity that the seeming misfortune had provided for me. I have often heard it said that it is not what happens to you that will determine your life's direction, but how you react to what happens to you. That was certainly true in my case. I remain grateful for my life. I would not trade my life for anyone else I know. And I thank God every day for the man He has allowed James Hanger to become.

# Chapter 59
## Another Hanger Limb Patent is Approved

I continued to develop new ideas for prosthetic limbs. My new invention related to improvements in attachments for the thigh-socket of my Hanger legs. It consisted of a clasp or fastener for readily attaching and detaching the artificial leg after it had been properly laced and tightened to the affected stump. The patent was filed on September 1, 1903 and accepted on June 14, 1904 as U. S. Patent No. 762,822.

The mechanism in Figure 2 was an interesting addition to the artificial limb. When a patient tied the laces tightly from Figure 1 through the holes in Figure 2, it enabled them to snugly attach and detach the prosthesis each morning and evening simply by pulling lever "d" up or down. I proudly think that little apparatus was one of my best ideas ever.

Where did James E. Hanger get all his ideas for U. S. Patent Office inventions? They all came from God. And I thanked Him every single night for those God-given talents.

No. 762,622.

PATENTED JUNE 14, 1904.

J. E. HANGER.
FASTENING DEVICE FOR ARTIFICIAL LIMBS.
APPLICATION FILED SEPT. 1, 1903.

NO MODEL.

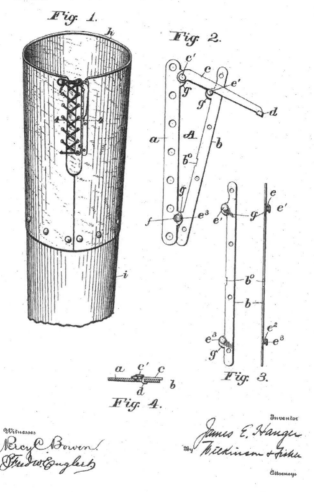

*Fig. 1.*

*Fig. 2.*

*Fig. 3.*

*Fig. 4.*

Witnesses
Percy C. Bowen
Fred W. Englerth

Inventor
James E. Hanger
by Wilkinson & Fisher
Attorneys

U.S. Patent Office

# Chapter 60
## My Retirement Kicks In

Our six boys, James Edward, Herbert Blair, Daniel McCarthy, Hugh Hamilton, Henry Hoover, and Albert Sidney, (we also had two daughters, Princetta Lee and Alice Rogers) had been involved in the business almost as soon as they were out of their diapers. They had learned early how to measure and fit a Hanger limb. I decided that they all needed to take their turn in the factory learning how to operate the machinery and build limbs. When I finally retired in 1905, though I continued to work for the company, my boys and my business managers took over the operations.

My assignment was to be president of the company, but I would only be available in an advisory capacity. My time from this day forward would be divided between being an elder in the Presbyterian Church and developing a long-range plan for the future of the company. It was also time for me to start working more seriously on my golf game.

I had worked tirelessly since the fall of 1861. After 44 years, I was thinking it was about time for old James Hanger, now 64 years old, to take a break and enjoy life. I really hadn't slowed down much during those years. But I really didn't feel like I was finished with my work either. I was always one to think tomorrow would bring more opportunities and greater challenges that would make Hanger limbs even better than they were today.

As I looked back to that first prosthetic limb that I made with barrel staves, I have to laugh. It was certainly crude by today's standards. But I had to start somewhere. It was 100 times better than Mike Sutton's peg leg or my Yankee peg leg. Yet it was also many times worse than the original Hanger patented limbs.

It had dawned on me recently that there are several things that I have overlooked in my assessment of the war that took my leg. One was that the bullets made of soft lead often shattered the bone and everything around it. This was a major cause for many of the 35,000 or so veterans who returned home dismembered in some fashion. It was also somewhat ironic that the Confederate soldier's political views (including supporting the South's agrarian economy) ended up with a disability that required a leg manufactured in a factory (the economy of the North).

I have also realized in my old age that all veterans missing a limb or several limbs who probably felt that they belonged to their military company or regiment during the conflict, suddenly felt that they didn't belong to anything when they went home.

As I looked forward to my retirement and taking Nora's advice to "smell the roses", I am certain Hanger limbs of the next fifty years or so will be much better too. And even if I am not around, the basic foundation of my company was built on a solid model of quality workmanship and expert service to those in need. My children knew the drill. They knew competitors have come and gone, but the Hanger name continued. They knew why the Hanger Company had maintained its edge. The concept was pretty simple – good old-fashioned customer service.

The Hanger Company had an outstanding track record. We had learned from our mistakes. We had listened to our customer's needs. We had offered quality prosthetic limbs for a good value. We were not always the cheapest priced limb, but that wasn't part of our goal. We have always stood by our workmanship. As certain as my name was James Hanger, I was also certain my boys and my managers would continue those traditions.

Our boys knew that no competitor could take that history away from them. They also had been taught to realize that if they started getting careless with the customers, those customers would go somewhere else. Customers always had a choice of where to purchase their limbs. At the Hanger Company, we knew we were not the only game in town. It was the Hanger way to make sure those customers were 100% satisfied. That assured us, in most cases, those people would not only continue to be our customers, but they would recommend us to others. Those referrals, in the long run, would always be our best form of advertising.

My only fear was that my children would not ask for my advice as I got older. Did I train them so well that they won't need their father anymore? I hoped this would not be the case.

By the end of 1906 and after considerable consultation from our attorneys, we incorporated and formed Hanger, Inc. Our plan was to continue to manufacture, sell, and repair artificial limbs and provide other supplies our customers would also need. The incorporation named me and my sons, James E. Hanger Jr. and Henry H. Hanger as principals. The corporation was initiated with three hundred dollars in stock certificates.

In the meantime, my golf game, no matter how hard I worked on it, was not improving. Sometimes it seemed the more I played that frustrating game, the worse I got. But my time outside on the golf course was never anything but peaceful, even when I was playing poorly. I would always contend that a day playing golf was never a bad day.

In spite of my retirement from the company, I continued to develop new prosthetic ideas and new inventions. I also watched as my boys filed their own patents for artificial limbs. I knew they would make me proud. God had blessed Nora and me with smart children.

My prayer was that they would conduct themselves in the manner in which I had taught them. I was confident that the Lord would lead them in the same manner that He had led me.

# Chapter 61
## Our Company was an Industry Leader

No other company could match us when it came to procedures for our customers. I have always maintained that our strength was knowing that our customer satisfaction was of paramount importance.

Every single limb was built to its wearer. We provided our Hanger limbs in a rough state first and let the customer try it out. "Rough state" to us meant that the limbs were put together but not finished, and as such, allowed us to make modifications to each and every single part. We could take a limb apart in a matter of minutes and make any required changes or adjustments.

As the customer tested their new limb, we would carefully watch and take notes, as I had back in Churchville in building and testing my very first Hanger limb.

What other companies did not realize fully was the testing period was totally governed by the physique of the wearer. No two were the same. A limb could never be adjusted or fitted just from measurements alone.

The muscles of the body were at rest when measurements were taken. But those same muscles react to the pressures exerted by a person's body, and change to a totally different mode when the person stands up and tries to take a step, engaging the artificial limb to full movement.

After the testing is successful, we take the limb back and complete building it to match the requirements observed in the trial.

The Hanger Company is the only manufacturer to allow this kind of practical testing while the limb is still in its rough form.

In a world made up of little things, attention to detail is something I have always insisted as being a high priority.

As I pray tonight, I ask God to make sure my sons remember these lessons as they continue to phase their father out of the business.

# Chapter 62
## Our Prize Winning Exhibit at the Jamestown Exposition

In 1907, the much promoted Jamestown Ter-Centennial Exposition was held in Norfolk, Virginia. Set up to commemorate the 300th anniversary of the founding of the Jamestown colony, this large fair offered visitors the opportunity to view many advances particularly in athletics and military prowess submitted by individuals, governments, and companies from twenty different countries. It was opened from April 26 until November 30. Hanger, Inc. set up a booth to show off our new designs. My sons, thinking I had nothing better to do, sent me on assignment to extoll the virtues of the company. I relished the opportunity to give up my retirement for that time at least.

Many dignitaries visited over the seven months of the exposition, bringing additional exposure to the exhibits at the fair. Those visitors included author Mark Twain, President Teddy Roosevelt and educator, Booker T. Washington.

Mr. Washington actually stopped by the booth and asked for me. He wanted to know if any colored men had been fitted with Hanger limbs. I told him absolutely. I explained that my company had no regard for the color of a man's war uniform or the color of his skin. I told him the story of the legless colored man from Washington D.C. who I had fitted for prosthetic limbs and who was now employed in my company as a janitor.

I told him I had also worked with Private Carr Hardy of the 7th U. S. Colored Troops. Hardy had his arm amputated following his wounding at Fort Harrison, Virginia in September, 1864.

I also explained that I employed colored men in my factories. Mr. Washington seemed pleased with the information that I had given him.

I was encouraged to submit the newest models of our company's Hanger Limbs in competition. My company received the First Grand Prize plus the Gold Medal for overall competition at the exposition.

In 1908, I chartered J. E. Hanger Inc. in superior court in Atlanta with my sons Herbert Blair and Albert Sidney as the other principals. Our capital stock set at $25,000 with the privilege to increase that to $100,000 if needed.

I thanked God for the opportunities my sons have made possible through their hard work. And for the blessings that all my children and grandchildren have brought into my life.

Ter-Centennial Exposition Medal
http://www.expomedals.com/1907

# Chapter 63
## The Passing of Nora

On April 3, 1909, my beloved wife and faithful partner, Nora, passed away at our new home at 1132 Lamont Street in Washington where we had just moved within the past year. We had been married since 1873 – a total of 36 years.

Never even once have I thought marrying Nora had been anything but a stellar decision on my part. My life was enriched by her holding my hand and supporting my work and my ideals from day one. She was a terrific wife, mother, business partner, and supporter. She was the compass that kept me on course throughout my life. Nora was the love of my life. May she rest in peace.

My sons and their families held me up in the weeks and months following as I languished in grief. And for some odd reason, at the same time, I grieved over the loss of my father, who I did not even remember.

My father, William A. Hanger, died in 1848, when I was just five years old. I had never really thought about how devastating that loss might have been for my mother as I was obviously too young to figure it out at the time. But enjoying my children as much as I had and then being with their families and my grandchildren, I thought it sad that my mother had to carry on without him. And that my father missed out on so much by dying so young.

I tended to take so much of life for granted. My son, Daniel McCarthy, tried to explain to me once or twice that it wasn't necessarily a solitary trait that only James

E. Hanger possessed. Of course, I had taken my leg for granted prior to it being lost. I certainly had taken Nora for granted though she knew she was loved and appreciated. I reminded her of that often. I just never expected to out-live her.

If I had those many wonderful years to do over, I probably would have not been at the company so long each day. I did tend to work too hard and too often. That wasn't because she pushed me. In fact, on most days Nora reminded me of my need to slow down and be patient. One of her favorite sayings was "if you can't help someone today, they will certainly still be there for you to help tomorrow." Her second favorite line was "James, it's time to stop and smell the roses."

As you might have guessed, even with all of the developments and improvements in my Hanger limbs over the years, I fell frequently. Nora knew that part of the process I had to go through was learning to pick myself up. She saw that I was determined and that she needed to allow me the liberty of trying to pick myself up without any help. Yet, at the same time, she was always hovering over me and offering me a hand. In the last few years, admittedly, I have needed her help to get up, after many long years of being too stubborn to allow her to help. But I did appreciate that she was always there for me, and told her that every single time.

Nora was also right about how the boys would handle the operations of the company. She declared often that it was no surprise to her that our sons' business practices topped mine tenfold. She knew that I was more interested in helping those in need than making money. The company was finally earning financial dividends not ever seen under my leadership.

That being said, we had really enjoyed my retirement years. She certainly loved all the grandchildren and they adored her. We would all miss her greatly.

My only prayer recently has been in gratitude for God's great wisdom in bringing Nora McCarthy into my life. A man could not have asked for a better wife. She was just another of God's constant parade of angels He has sent into my life over the years.

# Chapter 64
## Providing Non-War Related Prosthetic Limbs

Starting around 1870 and continuing into the 20$^{th}$ century, our prosthetic development and customer service treated more and more non-war related limb loss. Industrial accidents rose as more factories were built to produce products for the country. Mining and manufacturing led the way in industrial accidents, followed closely by the railroads.

The federal government and various states particularly in the northeast established regulations governing industrial safety. Even with those in place, accidents increased. I've seen reports that said "there is peril to life and limb from unguarded machinery" and "the workers have their risks of life and limb, of body and health...think of how many are crippled and maimed...for life in the service of capitol." It seemed to me that in their haste for workers to become more productive by using machinery, employers neglected the safety aspects of the work place. So while American workers produced more product than their counterparts around the world, they were also much more susceptible to injury.

Our corporate advertising strategy was to provide before and after photographs showing how Hanger limbs improved a person's life. In 1911, for instance, one of our advertisements showed a before photograph of double amputee, W. N. House, who had one leg missing above the knee and the other just above the ankle sitting in a chair wearing only a shirt. The after photograph showed Mr. House (an employee of the Baltimore and Ohio Railroad who lived in Magnolia, West Virginia) with Hanger limbs, standing tall, wearing a suit and holding a natty bowler.

Mr. House had the highest of praise for his Hanger limbs which he bragged he could wear up to thirty six hours without chaffing.

One of our largest customers during that time period was the vast Baltimore and Ohio Railroad.

Like all railroads, the Baltimore and Ohio Railroad had expanded greatly since the Civil War. And with its expansion came more and more business and an increase in employees. They began hauling freight with regularity. And the transferring of freight provided for more serious injury and dismemberment.

Baltimore and Ohio Railroad official S. R. Barr continually supported out company's efforts saying that they had received no complaints at all from the Hanger limbs we provided to their employees. He even ventured beyond that to tell us that although it was against his company's policy to recommend a particular artificial limb, his employees' choice of Hanger limbs continued to grow every single year.

Employees of the Baltimore and Ohio Railroad were not the only railroad employees to use Hanger limbs. In fact, our company was under contract with forty different companies including the Pennsylvania Railroad, The Norfolk and Western Railroad, the Carnegie Steel Company and others to provide for prosthetic limbs.

W. V. Higgins, yardmaster of the Macon, Dublin and Savannah Railway Company of Dublin, Georgia had a double slip-socket Hanger limb in 1905. By 1911, Mr. Higgins had received his second Hanger limb.

Walter Joseph Sylvia of Cordsville, South Carolina and an employee of the Southern Railways used a Hanger limb very successfully from his amputation from injury while working in 1905.

One of our smallest, youngest, and most successful customers came to us following his amputation in 1907. The customer was 4 years old. We fitted him with a Hanger limb.

The little boy who received the limb lived in Taylorstown, Virginia. His family reported that he used his crutches for just three weeks after receiving his artificial leg and then abandoned them to be able to use his Hanger limb without them.

We advertised regularly in such railroad publications as *The Railway Surgeon*, *The Railroad Trainman* and *The Brotherhood of Locomotive Firemen and Engineer's Magazine* touting our vast experience, our guarantee, and boasting that over 16,000 persons were wearing Hanger limbs. We suggested to all those readers that our limbs were "so natural in their action as to practically defy detection and relieve the wearers of the handicap of being considered crippled." You may recall, way back in 1861, it had been one of my specific aims – to help the person wearing the device stand in a line without being detected as the person missing a limb.

Our warranty was unlike any in the industry. It was listed in our advertising this way: "Each Hanger limb is warranted in writing for five years. That is, the artificial leg is to stand the same service as your natural leg barring accident, for a period of five years. We keep the limb in perfect walking order for this length of time."

Our slogans, as noted on the Hanger, Inc. letterhead were as follows: "Longest experience in the world making and wearing limbs" and "Quality remains after price is forgotten."

By this time I had also patents on the following items: lathe-fitted sockets, cordless knee joints, cordless ankle joints, flexible sockets for thigh amputation, and tapered bronze bushing knee joints. My company also provided the following services at our offices: rolling chairs, crutches, trusses, hospital and physicians supplies, and surgical instruments.

Our business was so brisk that we had outgrown our latest Washington, D.C. location. On September 1, 1911, we relocated to 221-223 G. Street NW, a prime location that was accessible by any of the principal car lines in the city. The new building was three stories and included a manufacturing facility, a showroom, and fitting rooms. My favorite part was a small basement where we intended to season black willow which had become one of the principal woods we were using in making Hanger limbs. Much of our black willow was harvested in West Virginia.

As I pray this day, I am reminded to thank God again for the opportunity He provided for me in losing my own limb in the war. Every one of these persons espousing their gratitude for their Hanger Limbs would not have been possible without God's direction and blessings.

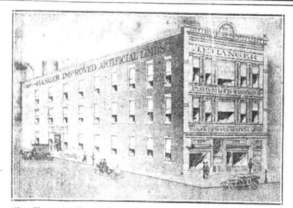

New Home of "Hanger Improved Limbs" in Washington. Other Factories in Atlanta and St. Louis.

# Removal Announcement

Owing to the enormous growth of our business, we have been compelled to secure larger quarters. The new Hanger factory, where we are now located, is equipped with the latest tools and machinery, and is the most up-to-date and complete factory in existence for the manufacture of

# ARTIFICIAL LIMBS

On direct line from heart of city to Union Station. All the principal car lines of the city will bring you to the door of our new offices, fitting rooms, and factory.

# J. E. HANGER, Third and G Sts. N W.

*Washington Post* September 3, 1911

218

# Chapter 65
## My Life without Nora

My life has definitely not been the same since I lost Nora in 1909. She really was my rock. Our children are certainly encouraging and supportive, but they have their lives, their positions with the company, and their families that take most of their time. They don't have much time for their father. Our large Washington house seems way too big for James Hanger without my Nora.

Nora was my steadiest influence. She was very even keeled. I needed that kind of support in my life.

I was much more technical, working more my hands. I'm thinking there were days smoke probably came out of my ears as the machinery for thinking spewed out the smoke from the ideas I concocted. At least she led me to believe that.

Nora, on the other hand, operated more on thinking, emotions, and the feelings side of things. In our case, the opposites functioned very well together.

Even with all that said, she would often look at my drawings and ask questions that were helpful. Her input resulted often in changes to the details.

She was always willing to add specific questions designed to make me think about something from perhaps a different angle. And she was always willing to work patiently to help this old dog perform some new tricks.

Not having Nora made a difference every single day. When I had an idea, I still wanted to bounce it off her and get her feedback. But she was not there.

Just like my missing leg, I had taken Nora for granted. Her presence was calming but certainly not unappreciated. I got used to her being there, leading the cheers for me, and always being supportive and positive. I didn't tell her enough how important she was to both my happiness and my success.

I laugh at the comparison, but Nora became like the "phantom pain" -- the itch in my foot that had not been attached for years. And as my body had been accustomed to its wholeness, my life had become accustomed to Nora.

My family, especially my grandchildren, often asked me to tell stories about their grandmother. My favorite was the time she was so angry with me (I don't even remember why) that she hid my Hanger limb. When I woke up that day, my leg was nowhere to be found. I thought that curious, since my artificial leg certainly had never gotten up and walked off on its own before. I hopped around the house, madder than a hornet, looking for it. And then I stopped and started laughing.

Nora came out of the kitchen and asked me what in the world I was doing. I explained that I was on the same mission little Samuel Hite had been on back in Philippi, Virginia in 1861 when he went looking for the leg I had lost. I had indeed lost my leg again. Only this time, I told Nora, it was not quite as painful as the first time.

Nora joined my search, half-heartedly, of course, since she knew very well where my lost leg had gone. The more I looked, the more she laughed -- with me, not at me. Finally she admitted that the leg that was "a missing" was in the ice box. Now it was my time to laugh again. I asked if she was keeping it on ice.

My grandchildren always liked that story the best.

That story always reminded me as to just how special Nora McCarthy Hanger had been in my life. I thank God every day that He allowed her to be my partner from so long. I missed her.

# Chapter 66
## Continuing to Improve my Hanger Limbs

My recent patent was a continuation of improvements on the artificial foot. It was filed in July of 1909 and accepted as U. S. Patent No. 951,989 on March 15, 1910. But I was still not finished.

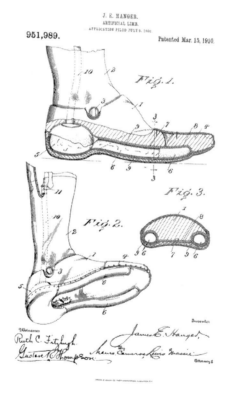

U.S. Patent Office

My next patent was filed July 24, 1911.

It was accepted on July 8, 1913 as U. S. Patent No. 1,066,605.

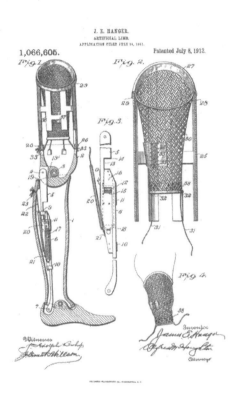

I followed that invention with another more complicated artificial leg on June 14, 1912. It included two drawings. It was accepted on August 26, 1913 and became officially U. S. Patent No. 1,071,230.

223

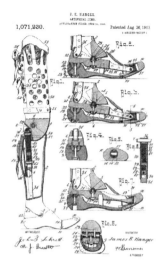

U. S. Patent Office

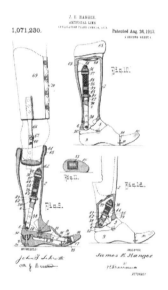

U. S. Patent Office

224

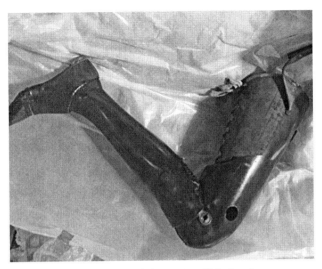

Hanger Limb – Philip J. Merrill Collection

Plate on limb shown above – Philip J. Merrill Collection

# Chapter 67
## Reminiscing about the Civil War

In 1914, I was asked to write about my Civil War service to help my daughter, Alice Rogers Hanger Cook, with her application into the United Daughters of the Confederacy, Virginia division. Here's some of what I recalled better now than when I first wrote about it.

*"Their columns were approaching Philippi from the west on two roads; the third column was to circumvent the town and cut off our retreat, in which they almost succeeded. The heavy roads and a little incident which I'll relate kept them from bagging our entire command. A pistol shot at or about 4:30 was to be the signal for the battery to commence firing. This battery had been placed on a high hill just west of the town about 2 o'clock that morning. As the Col. on the Clarksburg road passed old Mrs. Humphrey's home about 2 miles from Philippi just about daybreak, she started one of her boys to notify our command. Her boy was captured by some stragglers and she fired a gun at them. The commander of the battery took this for the signal and commenced firing about 4:20. He told me this. This firing was the first notice we had that the enemy was near us. The Col. Hint was to cut off our retreat was delayed some*

*30 or 40 minutes on account of heavy roads, which gave our forces time to get away.*

*The first two shots were canister and directed at the Cavalry Camps; the third shot was a 6 pound solid shot aimed at a stable in which the Churchville Cavalry Company had slept. This shot struck the ground, ricocheted, entering the stable and struck me."*

I have gone down this road many times in the last 53 years. Obviously with every other step I took I was reminded of my injury at Philippi. I was grateful that my daughter wanted to carry on the pride I have in my Confederate service, even though deep down inside I remained slightly embarrassed at the extreme brevity in the length of that service.

With the help of several of my sons, we added locations in population areas that were closer to a significant number of veterans needing our services. Those locations were Atlanta, St. Louis, Pittsburgh, Philadelphia, and Baltimore.

Each location included offices, a show room, a fitting room and in several instances, a factory. Veterans were encouraged to stop in and look at various prosthetic limbs. There were several rooms resembling dressing rooms someone would find in a department store for measuring, adjusting, and fitting artificial limbs for our customers. We also published a catalog they could take with them when they went back home.

At each location we also utilized display windows on the ground floor to show various Hanger limbs to anyone who might be walking by and would be able to look them over. We thought if someone who did not need an artificial limb was aware of our location, they might know someone who could use our services.

By this time, my son, James Jr., was involved in the National Comfort Chair Company in St. Louis, and the Cole Motor Car Company. He had several chair patents while at the same time running the Hanger Company operations there. He also patented a steering mechanism for vehicles and had a love for bicycles.

My son, McCarthy, while serving as Vice-President of the company, was at the same time operations manager of Andrew B. Graham Publishers and Lithographers of Washington, D.C.

As I thought back I was reminded that if that cannon ball would have struck differently, I may have died on the spot. I was very aware that God has been very good to James E. Hanger.

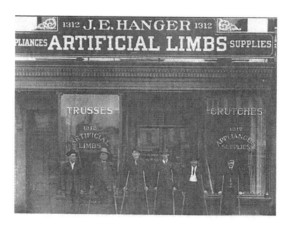

The Washington, D.C. office
http://civilwaref.blogspot.com/2013/02/james-edward-hanger-born-february-25.html

# Chapter 68
## Our Customers Give the Best Testimonials

In 1915, W. W. Horton who lived in Hillsboro, Illinois brought more praise to our company's work. He had received a Hanger foot in 1912. He indicated that he had never had one instance where the foot gave him any trouble He was a jitney driver and continued on with that occupation successfully.

As pleased as I always was to hear of the good work we were doing, I was even more pleased that Mr. Horton praised our Hanger service.

Another of our customers, Mr. R. C. Orr, wore a Hanger limb and then lost his other leg. He now had two Hanger limbs and through it all, he continued to ride his motorcycle.

Some testimonials come in other forms. Recently my son sent me an article in the *Atlanta Constitution* regarding an accident that is quite intriguing. I have quoted it here for you.

*A terrible accident happened on Whitehall Street yesterday morning just in front of the store of George Muse Clothing Company and when the men and women who thronged the thoroughfare at that time saw the sickening sight some blanched and others fainted.*

*An elderly gentleman of distinguished appearance and portly proportions slipped on a banana peel and fell. The cane on which he leaned slightly as he walked failed to stay his fall. It was seen that his right leg was double under him.*

*A score of willing hands were quickly raising the gentleman from the pavement and then it was seen that the limb had been crushed in the fall, for it hung as limp as if the bone had been crushed to bits. Several men rushed out from the Muse store to which the gentleman was carried. Someone telephoned an ambulance, and across the street George Adair, who had seen the accident, at once dropped everything and hastened to see if he could be of any aid.*

*Once the unfortunate man was in the store, Lloyd Parks, George Muse, Jr. and others connected with the establishment made efforts to alleviate his pain. Rugs and mats were laid on the floor and expensive clothing done into a wad to improvise a pillow.*

*But to the surprise of the rescuers, the gentleman would not lie of the bed prepared to him. He insisted on being given a chair. He was told that this would never due as he could not stand the pain. He still insisted and a chair was brought to him. With all admiring his nerve the gentleman settled in the chair, and then to the astonishment and relief of everybody, he pulled up his trouser leg and detached an artificial limb. And then he asked that it be carried to the J. E. Hanger Company from whom he had bought it in order that a newer limb might be fashioned in its stead.*

*The gentleman who went through this terrible experience as Judge A. C. Conn, of Canton, for many years ordinary of Cherokee County. While fighting for the Confederacy he received wounds which in the early eighties necessitated the amputation of the leg which those who saw him fall thought had been crushed into a pulp.*

*Though the laugh was on the crowd, the judge said he appreciated their kindness just as much as if his loss had been greater, and he was too much elated over the fact that it was not his good leg which had been smashed to grieve over the loss of one which was artificial.*

As grateful as my customers were to me, I was just as thankful of them for their willingness to provide testimony for my company even sometimes in the form of newspaper articles that put a smile on my face. And I thank God that I had been given my talent for invention.

## WHEN CORK LEG SNAPPED MEN AND WOMEN FAINTED

THEN HE BROKE—HIS CORK LEG.

*Atlanta Constitution*

231

# Chapter 69
## My European Trip

In 1915 I traveled to Europe. By this time it was pretty obvious that my sons did not need much advice from their "old man". And I must admit, since I split the business up between them, the operations had been running smoother than they ever had. In hind sight, perhaps I should have relinquished my leadership even earlier.

I had made appointments in various European cities. I was interested in studying modern amputation techniques and to see special adaptations that manufacturers in Europe were making with prosthetic limbs.

During my trip, I was surprised to be honored by British Royalty for my work in helping to rehabilitate England's veteran who had amputations.

Officials in England thought they may have had as many as 60,000 disabled soldiers. They gave me a tour of Queen Mary's Star and Garter Home, Sandgate, Kent, named after the queen who had thought it important to take care of their veterans. The facility was a place for dismembered veterans to rehabilitate and then do light jobs in the knitting industry. Their plan was to set up additional facilities around the country. They invited me to set up an artificial limb factory located right adjacent to the Queen Mary's facility which would become Hanger and Company Ldt.

One of our key employees, C. W. Thomas of our St. Louis factory, left to sail to Petrograd, Russia in July to meet with Russian officials to show them artificial limbs. Officials there had indicated to us that they were in the market for perhaps as many as 5,000 to supply their dismembered soldiers.

I also negotiated contracts with England and France and the American Red Cross to care for veterans from the recent world war.

The contract negotiated with England and France to provide artificial limbs totaled $15 million. The agreement called for shipping 250 limbs per month. The first shipment left our factory in Pittsburgh on October 4, 1915. Our Atlanta factory also provided shipments of Hanger limbs directly to England.

At this particular time, working double shifts, 250 limbs per month was our production limit. However, by the end of the year, we proposed to increase our output to between 1,200 and 1,500 limbs each month.

My trip certainly would have been more fun if Nora would have been there with me. We had always talked of traveling. Truthfully, I was never willing to take time off and like she said "smell the roses." Being in Europe and seeing all the sites alone reminded me of my phantom Nora itch – the one that remained, but that I could not scratch.

Having her see things with a different perspective had helped me greatly over the years. I missed that part from her too.

By the end of 1915, my sons had split J. E. Hanger, Inc. into four separate regional companies.

In July of 1916, I travelled back to Europe – this time to Paris, France with my sons Henry Hoover and Herbert Blair to see about the establishment of an artificial limb factory there. We rented a facility at 6 Rue

Edward VII. My sons found a place to stay and remained in France to operate at that location.

Each year I updated my city directory listings in the places we had companies by my adding to the number of years that I had worn a Hanger limb since 1861. As of this date in 1916, I have proudly worn one for 55 years. And for the last 55 years, I have thanked God every single day since that accident in Philippi, Virginia that He has allowed me to make something out of the misfortune that had found its way to me. So far that part is working out pretty well too. And He knows I am grateful.

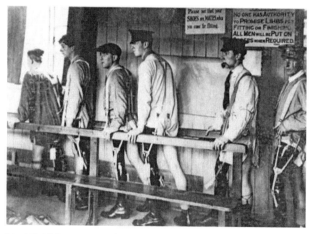

Disabled British veterans learning to walk again using Hanger limbs
Roehampton, England – 1916
http://storify.com/vasanthan/history-1

# Chapter 70
## World War Provides New Challenges

In 1917, the Artificial Limb Manufacturers and Brace Association (ALMBA) was formed. I was a founding member. Our purpose, supported by the Council on National Defense, was to prepare the industry for the influx of injured war veterans. We expected that the numbers would be staggering. The industry needed to be prepared from the repercussions that we predicted would not be that dissimilar to what we had gone through following the Civil War.

The organization was pressing to change the industry from manufacturers of prosthetics limbs to providers of professional care for the veterans as patients. They did not have to convince me of that. I had always thought the care of the patient, his comfort, and his well-being were significant and at least as important as the device that we were providing for him.

I was asked recently how my customers from the Civil War compared to my customers from the World War. I explained truthfully that although the wars and the procedures were quite different, the problems of disabled veterans had not changed one iota.

All veterans who were missing a limb had the same psychological struggles. They generally had lower self-worth than they would have had without their injury. They often were reclusive, in order to hide their disability. Many saw their infirmity as a calamity in their life rather than a challenge that certainly could be overcome. And for every veteran who accepted their prosthesis and tried to adapt it to their changed lives, there were always those who were not able to accept their fate and others who would choose not to wear an artificial limb.

Prosthetic limbs had improved greatly over the years. I was proud to have had a little something to do about that. Care for the veterans had also taken giant strides. Surgical techniques had come miles and miles since the day I was treated with no anesthetic and in less than sanitary conditions. Procedures that had been learned by trial and error in the Civil War and performed by people who in most cases had not even trained as surgeons were now taught by experienced medical personnel in institutions of higher learning. Surgeons of this modern era performed practice amputations on other animals as part of their training and their internships before they were allowed to deal with human patients.

Medical advancement in amputations gave us much more stable and accepting stumps with which to attach our artificial limbs. The stumps were generally more alike than different. A thousand Civil War amputations left me with a thousand different looking stumps.

The prosthetic limbs over the years did exactly what I had intended all along. They gave the wearer something that looked like their original limb but was also functional. And more importantly, when someone observed my customers, their eyes did not go directly to their artificial limb.

In August, I was able to secure a contract for a permanent display of Hanger limbs to be shown by the Southeastern Exhibit Association at the Blosser Bulding in Atlanta. The association was set up to showcase products from many industries manufactured in the region surrounding the city.

By 1918, our firm's advertising in the Pittsburgh City Directory touted the fact that 60,000 persons worldwide were now wearing Hanger limbs. While that seemed utterly amazing to me, I was also quite proud that my little "opportunity" back in 1861 had turned into a thriving business opportunity which included employment of my family and some of their family members. I prayed that my sons would continue that fine tradition.

ALMBA founding members
Mr. Hanger is 4th from the left in the front row
Photo provided by American Orthotic and Prosthetic Association

James E. Hanger from photo above

Hanger Co. Factory Washington, DC
Largest plant in America – March 8, 1918
©Bettmann/CORBIS

Hanger Limb Factory
1917
Bob O'Connor Books archives

J. E. Hanger Artificial Limb Co.
Probably of Pittsburgh factory
National Photo Company Collection

# Chapter 71
## My Recent Years

May 10, 1919

As the years have gone by, my sons have been able to carry on mostly without me. I have become the wise old man who they could come to in case they had to have that one question answered that only their father would know. Their requests lately have been very infrequent. I was proud of their management skills. They continued to live the goals that I had tried so hard to establish.

As I look back on my life, I had these thoughts: "Science and invention have done, and are doing, more to cancel your misfortune than can possibly be done for any other serious handicap in life."

"Today I am thankful for what seemed then to be nothing but a blunder of fate, but which was to prove instead to be a great opportunity."

I truly believed that what made my work ultimately more important beyond just my own personal life was because the world failed to grasp the needs of thousands of veterans who had lost limbs. Artificial limb manufacturers had too long been more interested in manufacturing limbs and receiving government funds than they were in finding out how to actually help their individual customers.

I know my days are numbered. My children and grandchildren stay close by. These last few weeks I have been too ill to leave the house. I hadn't played golf in several years, even though that had become a simple pleasure in my life.

Often my thoughts turned back to that event in Philippi, Virginia on June 3, 1861 that had shaped every single day of my life ever since. What might have been life's ultimate curse for James E. Hanger, of the Churchville Cavalry, had actually been one of God's amazing blessings. Who would have thought?

I could not have imagined while lying on that hard bench in the United Methodist Episcopal Church, that anything could have been salvaged of my life in the not too distant future. Or that one man who had his natural limb taken in an instant, or in Dr. Robison's case, in 45 minutes, could have contributed productively to this vast world.

My position today was not much different than it had been in my last 58 years, in being eternally grateful to God for allowing me to respond to His challenge in such a positive way.

My situation can be summed up as follows: "From the efforts of a one-legged man with a crudely designed substitute for the leg lost in the war, the concern which bears my name has grown into the world's foremost manufacturer of artificial limbs."

If I were to write my own epitaph it would be simply this. "Here lies James E. Hanger – a man who made the best of a bad situation."

My evening prayer this day was to thank God for all the wonderful angels he has brought into my life including but not limited to Nora, Dr. Robison, Dr. New, Deborah, the Hite and McClaskey families, my children and grandchildren and many more. I am truly blessed.

# Chapter 72
## Visiting in Washington

June 15, 1919

*As told by a visitor*

I had written the family and asked if I could visit. I asked them not to tell Mr. Hanger when I would be arriving because I had not known exactly myself. It depended on my ability to make the proper connections. I had traveled from West Virginia by train to see him at his home in Washington, D.C.

When I arrived on this Sunday morning, his son, James Jr., greeted me. He said his father was asleep. We chatted informally. I told him that my family had treated his father while he was convalescing in Philippi, following his amputation and that we had kept in touch.

James told me he had been familiar with the story because his father had told the family of his little friend, Samuel Hite. That revelation made me feel truly grateful.

After talking for a while, James led me upstairs to his father's bedroom. We entered. Mr. Hanger was asleep. His son told me he had work to do. He asked me to wait here until his father woke up. He left and closed the door.

I looked around. I saw Mr. Hanger's artificial leg on the table -- the famous Hanger limb. I examined it quietly, turning it over in my hands. It was so much more advanced that the leg he had shown me in 1881. I was not surprised. His whole life had been devoted to perfecting something artificial when a cannon ball took away the leg that God had made for him.

I admired so much what Mr. Hanger had done. As a little boy, a stranger came into our house. I took a liking to him. He only had one leg. I was a curious boy, age 6. When he told me he had lost his leg, I foolishly went looking for it. I hated the peg leg they had given him. He didn't stay very long at our house, but to this little boy, he had made a profound impression.

I cried for days after he left. I had asked him to please come back. I never dreamed that he would. I should have known he would not forget me. He visited our family back in 1881.

When I learned what Mr. Hanger had done after he left Philippi, I was greatly impressed. I thought often that a lesser man would have gone home and felt sorry for himself. He might have locked himself in his house and never come out. But not Mr. Hanger. He went home and started making a difference, one veteran at a time. He had touched so many people over the years, perhaps thousands. To me, he was certainly a very special man.

When he finally woke up, I called his name. "Mr. Hanger. Mr. Hanger. Are you awake?"

"Who is it? I cannot see you. Come closer to the bed. Who are you?"

"It's Samuel. Samuel Hite."

He seemed confused. He certainly wasn't expecting a visit from me. He looked around like he couldn't see me. I am not sure he would have recognized me anyway. It had been almost 40 years since he had visited. I had not seen him since. "Say your name again. I am not sure I heard you right."

I walked toward the bed. I spoke louder. "Samuel. Samuel Hite from Philippi, Virginia. Do you remember me?"

He seemed stunned, like he couldn't believe his ears. Or that he might be dreaming. He looked around, staring but perhaps not seeing me. I was thinking in his old age he might have been confused. Or maybe he did not remember who I was.

I didn't know what to do. I just waited.

Slowly Mr. Hanger sat up and reached into the pocket of his robe. He pulled out a little crooked metal cross, the one that I had made for him with my father and the local blacksmith's help back in 1861. He held it up. I reached up and took his hand, cradling it in mine, with the cross in the middle. Our hands locked tightly. Tears ran down his face and mine.

"Samuel," he said. "Samuel Hite." He took another breath and struggled to speak. "I certainly do remember you." He paused again. And then he slowly added, "I have prayed on this cross every single night of my life."

It wasn't but a few minutes later that I felt his hand let go. He was gone. Mr. Hanger, my lifelong friend, had breathed his final breath. Once again I had not wanted him to go.

James E. Hanger

Hanger grave at Glenwood Cemetery in Washington, D.C.
Section F Range B Site 903

# Epilogue

James Hanger died on Sunday, June 15, 1919. He was 76 years old.

His funeral was held on Tuesday afternoon, June 17 at the West Street Presbyterian Church in Washington, D. C. He was buried at the Glenwood Cemetery next to his beloved wife, Nora.

At the time of his death, the company that he founded had business locations in London, England and Paris, France as well as in Atlanta, Baltimore, St. Louis, Pittsburgh, Philadelphia and Washington, D.C.

During the next seventy years, the company was split into independent offices, operated by Mr. Hanger's sons and several sales managers. They continued to support each other, with patients who received a limb from one office able to have updates or service at any other office. For many years the offices operated with one brochure and shared exhibit space at major trade shows. His sons and his company employees continued to patent new improvements in artificial limbs.

In 1996, J. E. Hanger Inc. was purchased by Hanger Orthopedic Group, Inc., for $49 million in cash and stocks, creating the country's largest producer of orthotic and prosthetics.[1]

Today the company operates as Hanger, Inc. and is a member of the New York Stock Exchange (HGR). It is the country's largest provider of prosthetics and orthotics

---

[1] http://www.nytimes.com/1996/07/30/business/company-news-hanger-orthopedic-in-deal-for-j-e-hanger.html

to over one million patients annually. The company operates over 740 patient care clinics in the United States. They also employ a significant number of physically challenged employees.

And they still honor and abide by the tenets articulated by the company's founder, James Edward Hanger, who always believed the following: "There is sound logic in our determination not to extend our activities beyond our capacity. If we have learned no other lesson, we are fully convinced of the wisdom of the policy we have followed all these years, never to allow our output to grow faster than our standards of quality and individual attention will allow."[2]

Retired Sgt. Bill Dunham and Hanger, Inc. Business Development Manager, himself an amputee from the U. S. invasion of Panama in 1989, talked recently about the company's founder, James E. Hanger. "To fabricate your own prosthesis because no one else was capable of doing it, you've got to think about what was going through his mind. What James Hanger did," Dunham continues, "really shows how people find ways to overcome the things life handed them. It shows the human spirit is pretty amazing."[3]

Ivan Sabel, former CEO and Chairman of Hanger, Inc. said that "The name Hanger is to prosthetics as the name Kleenex™ is to tissues. In this industry, everyone knows that with that name comes a lot of responsibility to quality and public service."[4]

---

[2] The Hanger Story, www.hanger150.com
[3] Hanger – 150 Years of Empowering Human Potential, pg. 33.
[4] http://occupational-therapy.advanceweb.com/editorial/content/printfriendly.aspx?CC=1 27026

The company also continues its charitable contributions. Following the war in Viet Nam, they donated over 9,000 prosthetic limbs and staff to the Viet Nam Assistance for the Handicapped (VNAH).

In 2005, the company donated $250,000 over a five year period toward the formation of the J. E. Hanger College of Orthotics and Prosthetics in St. Petersburg, FL which is obviously named after the company's founder.[5]

Following the Haiti earthquake in 2010, Hanger, Inc. provided $250,000 in funding and orthopedic devices to assist with the medical needs of those affected by the earthquake. They also established the Haiti Amputee Coalition and a long-term prosthetic and rehabilitation center in Deschapelles, Haiti.[6]

The 2011 movie "Dolphin Tale" starring Morgan Freeman is the story of a bottlenose dolphin that had been injured and was fitted with an artificial tail designed and developed by Hanger, Inc.

In 2013, Hanger, Inc. pledged a $100,000 educational grant to support the Amputee Coalition's Improving the Well-Being of People with Limb Loss program.[7]

The Hanger, Inc. company vision embodies the spirit of its founder, James E. Hanger, even today, that being "to be the partner of choice for service and products that enhance human physical capability."

The goal of the company's clinical staff is as it has been since 1861, to assist all persons in reaching their

---

[5] http://www.oandp.com/articles/news_2006-04-27_01.asp
[6] Hanger, Inc. Philanthropic Efforts fact sheet
[7] Hanger, Inc. Philanthropic Efforts fact sheet

highest possible level of independence so that their quality of life is enriched on a daily basis.[8]

All this happened because in 1861, a Confederate soldier struck down by a wayward cannonball and who was given "lemons", decided to make lemonade! Thanks to his response to his own personal life altering moment and his determination to make a difference, the world as we know it is a much better place. And as of 2013, James E. Hanger has certainly made huge amounts of lemonade and shared it with the world, one patient at a time.

In my mind, James E. Hanger is the most significant hero today to have participated in the American Civil War.

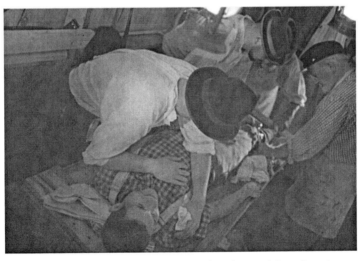

Hanger amputation reenactment at the Blue and Gray Reunion
Held annually in May
Conducted by "doctor" Noel Clemmer (right)
www.blueandgrayreunion.org

---

[8] http://wesclark.com/jw/first_amputee.html

# Additional notes

The only fictitious persons in this book are Deborah and Mike Sutton, who are composite characters. Every other person in the book is a real character.

The United Methodist Episcopal Church in 1861 was the only place of worship in Philippi. The building was used by all denominations for services. The federal government later reimbursed the church $700 for damages caused during the war. The church building was taken down circa 1890. The Philippi Baptist Church stands on that same site today.

Philippi, Virginia became Philippi, West Virginia in 1863 with the formation of the 35th state. The town's official and proper name originally was Phillippa as designated in 1843, and was not actually changed to Philippi until 1869.

Left to right – Howard Carswell, James E. Cook III and the author at
the historical marker in Churchville and across the street from where
James E. Hanger's home had been
Photo by Arlen Hanger

## <u>Good Reads on this Subject</u>

Hasegawa, Guy R. – "Mending Broken Soldiers, The
Union and Confederate Programs to Supply Artificial
Limbs", Southern Illinois University Press, Carbondale,
Illinois, 2013

Herschbach, Lisa Marie – "Fragmentation and Reunion:
Medicine, Memory and the Body in the American Civil
War", doctoral thesis, Harvard University, 1997

Houser, Donald W, Jr. – "Remembering the Churchville
Cavalry" – Publish America, Frederick, Maryland, 2011

Parks, Bob – "Hanger – 150 Years of Empowering
Human Potential" -- Metcher Media, 2012

## <u>Good Places to Visit on this Subject</u>

Blue and Gray Reunion, Philippi, WV – Hanger amputation reenactment – last weekend in May each year

National Civil War Medical Museum, 48 E. Patrick Street, Frederick, Maryland

# Acknowledgements

Hardy thanks for the cooperation and support of Hanger, Inc. coordinated from their corporate press office through Jennifer Bittner and Krisita Burket. Kudos also to Kevin Carroll, Hanger, Inc. Vice-President of Prosthetics, who met with me to discuss this project. And to McCarthy Hanger III, a great grandson, who is still active in the industry today. Mr. Hanger III provided me with valuable information for my book. Their cooperation greatly aided me in my writings.

I am grateful to Harold Carwell of Churchville, VA who has worked hard over the years to keep the legend of James E. Hanger alive in his hometown. Included in Mr. Carwell's work was the dedication of the James Hanger historical marker in Churchville on July 11, 1998 by members of the United Daughters of the Confederacy and the Churchville Historical Society. Hanger Orthopedic Incorporated officials also participated. Mr. Carwell and Arlen Hanger spent some time with me recently, helping me to try to understand the ins and outs of Churchville. Your efforts are greatly appreciated.

David Dufficy deserves special commendations for his contribution to this book.

Thanks to Barbara Collins, great granddaughter of James E. Hanger and descendant of Princetta Hanger, for providing me with information her family had collected. A grateful note also goes to Cal Hanger Jones, great, great grandson of James E. Hanger, who also provided helpful information on the Hanger family.

James F. Cook III, another great grandson who descended from James E. Hanger's daughter, Alice, provided me with the photograph of Mt. Hope, something many of us have been searching for, and a photograph of a Hanger Limb.

Congratulations to the officials of the Blue and Gray Reunion, Philippi, West Virginia for supporting the reenactment of the Hanger amputation held annually and for providing a forum for this event to be recognized and remembered. And to "doctor" Noel Clemmer who performs the Hanger amputation reenactment, thereby informing and teaching us about Civil War surgery and medicine. Thanks also for information provided by Lucretia Moyer, secretary of the Philippi Baptist Church.

I appreciate Eric Boyle, archivist, National Museum of Health and Medicine for his prompt retrieval and access to the General Daniel Sickles lithograph from the Otis Historical Archives. Thanks to Terry Reimer, Director of Research, National Museum of Civil War Medicine in Frederick, Maryland and Crystal Smith, Reference Librarian, History of Medicine Division, for their help and patience in allowing me to search for what I needed in their archives.

I would also like to take time out to thank Eileen Parris and the archivists at the Virginia Historical Society and the helpful personnel at the Virginia Public Library, both in Richmond, for aiding my research. I appreciate the research of Beth S. Harris, Special Collections & Government Information Librarian, Wyndham Robertson Library, Hollins University for information on Nora McCarthy Hanger who attended Hollins Institute 1867 through 1868.

Thanks to Tina Moran and Don DeBolt of the American Orthotic and Prosthetic Association for providing the photograph of the founding fathers of the ALMBA.

I was lucky to have connected with Mike Wood who has tons of information on the 16th Ohio Volunteer Infantry on his website www.mkwe.com. His data on Dr. James Robison was quite helpful.

I am very grateful in finding Philip J. Merrill of Baltimore. Philip has a collection of over 30,000 artifacts which included a Hanger leg. Thank you Philip for connecting with me and allowing me permission to use the photographs I have included.

I am blessed with the daily support I get from my family and friends. Two people stand out because they have been there for me every single day for years and years and years – my daughter, Kelli, and my sister, Joanne. Several others were particularly important to this project including Debbi Pierce, Jim Teague, and Ron Zeitz. You keep me going and keep me smiling.

And to my author friends and my Publishing 101 students (current and past) who know what I go through on a daily basis. Stand up and take a bow!!

Thanks to Rebecca Boreczky, the teacher who got me started to finally publish "The Perfect Steel Trap Harpers Ferry 1859" when I took her publishing class in Westminster, Maryland in 2005. I continue to be grateful for her encouragement.

I am always appreciative to those who continue to purchase and read my books. With over 9,700 sales to date and now ten books in print, my readers stretch from Charles Town, West Virginia, all the way to Afghanistan and most everywhere in between. I am also very thankful to those organizations, businesses and events who continue to offer me venues to speak, appear, sell, and sign books.

Here's the deal. If you keep buying and reading my books, I'll keep writing more. I appreciate every single one of you. God bless

CPSIA information can be obtained
at www.ICGtesting.com
Printed in the USA
FFOW04n0042191017
41281FF